After leaving teaching Margaret Stead studied Art in Harrogate and was a practising and exhibiting artist for ten years. She then returned to academic study, gaining an M.A. in Art History at the former Leeds Polytechnic and a Ph.D. in History at the University of Leeds. She has published several articles and collaborated with her husband, Geoffrey Stead, in writing *The Exotic Plant: a history of the Moravian Church in Great Britain, 1742-2000* (Epworth Press, 2003).
They still live in Yorkshire.

The Quiet Vale

Margaret Stead

The Quiet Vale

AUSTIN MACAULEY

A CIP catalogue record for this title is
available from the British Library.

ISBN 978 1 84963 011 5

www.austinmacauley.com

First Published (2010)
Austin & Macauley Publishers Ltd.
25 Canada Square
Canary Wharf
London
E14 5LB

Printed & Bound in Great Britain

For my family

ACKNOWLEDGEMENTS

I would like to thank the staff of
Austin and Macauley for all their work,
particularly Shannon Lynam and Katherine Kot
who co-ordinated the production and marketing
of the book, and Krysia Winska, the proof reader,
whose care and attention to detail I much
appreciated. Any remaining errors are
my responsibility.

I am grateful, also, to my grand-daughter, Jacqui
Tye, for designing the cover illustration; three
generations of our family remember the
school well.

Above all, I have appreciated the untiring interest
and support of my husband.
Thank you, Geoff, for all those rewarding
conversations and sustaining lattes in our
favourite coffee shops.

Prologue

I will arise and go now, for always night and day
I hear lake water lapping with low sounds by the shore;
While I stand on the roadway, or on the pavements grey,
I hear it in the deep heart's core.

From W. B. Yeats, *The Lake Isle of Innisfree*

If I can unlock a door in my mind and walk out into a village I once knew, perhaps I can finally understand the restless longing and sense of loss which are the background to my happy days. It was a world such as Dylan Thomas described in *Fern Hill*, when 'Time let me play and be / Golden in the mercy of his means', a world of scents and sounds and textures, of things growing, of keen sweet air, before the coming of the tractor, before the plague of weed-killer and pesticides. Horses pulled carts full of hay, corn, sugar-beet, turnips, grazed after work in flower-rich pastures which had never known the plough, and raised curious heads to blow a gentle greeting to evening strollers through moist, quivering nostrils; March hares cavorted, partridges whirred up from ploughed land, and skylarks rose singing into the sky until they passed beyond sight and only the sound lingered on. Rooks cawed, flocks of lapwings called a plaintive 'pee-wit' over the fields, and parties of yellowhammers fluttered fussily in the hedgerows.

It was a world of the senses for which no words are adequate, unmediated through adult eyes. Unexpected glimpses bring me close to tears: a television interview with someone living in peace on Lindisfarne; grazing cattle or horses glimpsed from a train; a close-cropped field with a few mature trees; a marshy patch with hoof prints, rushes and a pond in the corner; the scent of wild roses rioting in summer hedgerows; blackberries fragrant and juicy, or clustered hawthorn berries gleaming red in autumn among their turning leaves.

Was it the land of lost delight? No, because I don't long to be a child again. The village I knew exists only in the vulnerable, four-dimensional world of memory, but it resonates as a counterpoint to everyday experience. It is still there in name, the remaining old cottages gentrified beyond recognition, gardens and orchards of old fruit trees cleared away, their names forgotten and their space desecrated by small estates of modern houses. Who now remembers purple plums with the evocative name of 'cobbler balls', Keswick and codling apples, golden hazel pears? What I wish to recapture is a way of looking, a delight in savouring simple things. Possibly, by doing so, I can understand why memory with its richness, sensitivity and joy, is inseparable from longing and pain. I'll try to recreate that world, partly for sheer pleasure, partly to share with you the life of one village and what it was like to be me, a child there in the late 1920s and early 1930s.

A significant part of becoming aware of my small place in this country idyll was the gradual acceptance that I was different from others who lived there, which I was never allowed to forget; we came from elsewhere; we were not village people. My mother inundated me with her mother's sayings, tales of her wonderful older sister, Gert, who taught her in the infants' school, her schooldays at Castleford Grammar School when Henry Moore was there as a pupil, college days at Bingley Training College during the First World War. As a captive listener, at first sitting on her knee, later in fireside chats, I almost lived her experiences; they were her cherished past, because her mother and sister both died before I was four years old and, in her bitterness and loss, she found scant enjoyment in everyday life in a small village, a newcomer and too much aware of her perceived position as the schoolmaster's wife. I was audience to her idealized recollections of a childhood in which she visited her aunt and uncle who farmed at Norton, near Doncaster, and had kittens she could play with. She and her mother went there by train; the boys, Ernest and Harry, walked with their father to save train fares. Separateness was ingrained in her family tradition: they stood apart from the main mining community, remembering a more affluent past on her mother's side as local pottery owners who had status and were prominent Wesleyans. Her father, George Beach, came as a migrant worker from Gloucestershire, probably in the early 1870s, and worked at a colliery as a 'hanger-on', responsible for weighing and recording the coal mined by each team, the basis for calculating their wages, since they were paid according to the team's production. My mother delighted in repeating that he was not open to influence and had the reputation of being 'the fairest man in the pit'.

My grandmother, Lydia, had been trained as a dressmaker and her mother was a milliner; so, in pursuit of the best achievable future for her daughters, she wanted both of them to train as teachers and not to have to 'earn a living by the needle'. Gert, ten years older than my mother, trained in the classroom and at a pupil-teachers' centre, but my mother was young enough to benefit from a different system. As a sixth-former in the grammar school she took the Cambridge Senior examination and did some teaching practice in local schools, so qualifying for a place at the new teacher-training college for women at Bingley. Her family indoctrination involved speaking well, dressing well, and having good manners and deportment. It only partly succeeded with the boys; instead of at least one of them becoming a clergyman as their mother hoped, Ernest trained as a confectioner and Harry became a skilled cabinet-maker, who made suites of furniture for a local firm and did some restoration work in churches, but, thanks to two world wars, never had the means or opportunity to set up his own business.

One thing I regret is that, while my father was alive, I had no means of recording the stories he told about his early life in the Calder Valley. He shared with us his village childhood and youth in anecdotes full of fun and caricature, where the characters came back in late-Victorian rectitude, rivalry and ribaldry. We laughed uproariously whenever he imitated the village dialect and brought to life the worthy or less reputable men and women who lived in Mytholmroyd during the last decade of Queen Victoria's reign. It was a close community then, set around its few mills in the heart of the Pennines, almost on the Lancashire border, and my father's family were local people and part of it. As in the case of my mother's family, there was wealth on his mother's side, and status, too, as the local community measured it, in his case not in times past, but in the present, as three of his mother's sisters were connected with textiles, one by marriage to a mill-owner and two because they moved to Cardiff to set up in business. My grandmother, the eldest daughter, became pregnant before her eighteenth birthday and had to marry the culprit, Isaac Nicholl, the eldest son of a local hill farmer, who became a wool waste merchant with a room at the mill, through the kindness of wealthier members of his wife's family. He had a congenitally weak heart and couldn't do heavy work, dying in his early sixties. 'Our poor Sarah Elizabeth' was pitied and patronized by the rest of the family, but their four children all did well. Connie, the eldest, who never married, trained as a tailoress; John went to a technical college in Halifax and became a painter and decorator with his own successful decorating business and shop in Mytholmroyd; Chrissie, the youngest, reputed to be very intelligent, qualified as a teacher, but married an accountant, Arthur Allwright, before she had worked, and settled in London.

My father, the third child, also a potential pupil-teacher, was allowed to assist in teaching the younger children in the local school when he was eleven. By the time he was fourteen he was teaching juniors and, like Gert, training at a pupil-teachers' centre. In 1911, aged twenty-four, he had an opportunity to convert his teaching qualification to certificated status by spending a year in college, and went to the Methodist Training College in Westminster. Half the diary of his year in London survived my mother's search to destroy it as soon as he died. She tore up and burned the second exercise book, which I had often read with pleasure. This contained the most interesting records of being out and about in London, but it also included a tender account of his friendship with a girl called Molly, ending with their farewells and promise they would never introduce each other to the person they married. My father knew that he would be expected to return to Yorkshire and provide for his mother and two unmarried sisters; so he applied for a job with the West Riding. This took him to Castleford, where he bought a house for them all in Smawthorne Lane near my grandparents' home, and there he met a pretty schoolgirl, Beatrice Beach, whom he married ten years later, after the intervention of the First World War and a long engagement because of his other commitments.

Some of his reminiscences have faded from my memory, but a few remain, tantalizing me with half-memories, revealing now the boy he was, the man he became, the father I loved and under-valued when he was alive. I wish they had been recorded; I wish he had lived long enough to regard me less authoritatively as an adult in my own right, not just the 'little daughter' he still imagined me to be, and for me to mature to the point where I could overcome my irritation with his didactic manner and talk to him person to person. His version of his wartime experiences, sensitively edited for his 'little wife' and child, lead me to think he would have shared his feelings about this and many other things in a way I rarely glimpsed; but I never asked. He was a thoughtful man with a philosophical cast of mind, who kept his real feelings to himself, but the comforting, optimistic, caring person I knew provided solace to a child only too vulnerable to her mother's fretfulness and discontent. I loved to escape into my own outdoor world, but I preferred his comfortable, practical demonstration of horticultural skills to the chores of domesticity. Both my parents will emerge from the story as I tell it, not without prejudice, but as honestly as memory will allow.

Perhaps already our ephemeral society, where e-mails are so much more convenient than letters, is beginning to generate its own nostalgia for the past. Personal records of simple family life in a changing world become fascinating once the culture that shaped them has gone, even though they say little more than, 'this is how we lived'. When we are involved in our working and family lives we regard ourselves as the present generation, moving forward, and under-value the experience of our elders. Then, one day, as I well know, we realize that the people we loved and took for granted are gone, and their memories with them. I believe, then, that I have something significant to share before it is too late, simple and personal though it may be.

So how do I begin? What is the best way to pass on my recollections of the village in which I was a child? The historian who has recently taken over from the simpler soul who let life take its course is tempted to analyse and depersonalize the task. Should I delve seriously into old records? There is manuscript material about the neighbourhood in the Yorkshire Archaeological Society's archive at Claremont in Leeds and, before diverting into art history, I read and made notes from old court records of Upper Dunsforth, I noted quarrels about beaten wives and stolen pigs, dipped into controversies that divided the Ouseburns during the Civil War, and began to read material about Thorpe Underwoods which nobody had researched; it could probably be blended with reminiscences into something of wider interest than personal recollections alone. I shan't go down that road; I no longer want to challenge my eyesight by reading seventeenth-century script on vellum, though I love those old documents and their language, and the older village life of tofts and crofts, in which one, John Coates, bought a parcel of land... and so on.

It's no good pretending that my child's eyes saw the village and its people as others would who grew up as part of the farming community. It would be better just to write as a young observer and let the observations be the story from which these people will emerge. A few adults were part of my daily life and I knew others and savoured them with a shrewdness which often surprises me in retrospect. I'll just record what I remember and let it speak for itself. It's our family's story, too, part of where they come from. I shall enjoy the adventure of recalling the unique insights of a child.

PART I

A VILLAGE CHILDHOOD

CHAPTER I
The village and the school house

Throughout my childhood my life was centred on Great Ouseburn, a village in the Vale of York, set on a gently rounded terminal moraine laid down by the retreat of a glacier at the end of the last Ice Age. The houses are separated from the 'high road', the Roman road between Eboracum and Isurium, now York and Aldborough, by carr land that winds through the valley between Great Ouseburn and Kirby Hall park. It is useful only as seasonal rough grazing and provides a channel for the Ouse Gill Beck, which rises in the grounds of the old workhouse and is fed by several other springs running down the hillside behind the village. At one end of the village, beyond the village green, lies another area of marshy ground, the Seggans (sedge ings), alongside which a narrow road leads to Upper Dunsforth, which stands on its own terminal moraine and in turn is backed by extensive carrs, now believed to be the result of a 'kettle hole', an area of land beneath which ice was trapped for centuries after the retreat of the ice, melting slowly and causing the ice to sink. This land is now a Site of Special Scientific Interest, owned by our family, leased to and managed by the Yorkshire Wildlife Trust as a nature reserve; but that's not part of the present story.

At the other end of Great Ouseburn, Boat Lane branches off to the left, skirts Kirby Hall Park and, a mile further on, crosses the River Ouse into the old North Riding via Aldwark Bridge, still a privately owned toll bridge. The main road between the villages crosses the 'fish-pond bridge' and passes Little Ouseburn church and Moat Hall. Beyond this, Little Ouseburn village street branches off to the right, leading to the high road, and the

21

through road continues to Thorpe Underwoods, with its old grange that once belonged to Fountains Abbey and, alongside the grange, Thorpe Underwoods Hall, where Anne Bronte was employed and Branwell Bronte worked as tutor. The road then curves round to join the high road at a junction with the road to Whixley. All the villages, therefore, lie along roads that lead back to the old Roman road. In the 1930s, unmade lanes with high hedgerows, footpaths and rights of way gave access to fields and outlying farms behind the villages and down to the river and provided time-honoured short cuts across farm land between the villages. Some of these remain, as do the farms, while others have been lost to mechanization and the consequent enlargement of fields.

In July, 1926, my father moved from Castleford to a new job as headmaster of Great Ouseburn village school and my parents went to live in the school house, so joining a community that had been tied to the land for centuries and had changed little in character. I went along as well, but *incognito* until September. The school took all the children aged five to fourteen from Great and Little Ouseburn, Upper Dunsforth, Branton Green and Thorpe Underwoods, around one hundred, varying by five or six either way. At that time Miss Dawson taught the infants, Miss Coupland the juniors and my father the seniors. The school house adjoined the school, but the former access door had been blocked up. Our back yard, the surrounding garden, and the playgrounds out of school hours, were where I played, with the added freedom to roam in Jacksons' field, the grazing land that surrounded the school on three sides; the front of the house faced the village street.

Across the field was a small, enclosed spinney and the 'sewerage', a mass of wide pipes and scummy, stinking sewage beds, the workings of which were a mystery, but they drained effluent from the farms. The water from the village pumps was pure and wholesome, because it came straight from a large underground lake. Cold and refreshing, it tasted of the limestone over which it lay. Our drinking water came from a pump in the boys' playground. At playtime, sweaty boys ran to the pump to drink and wet their heads and dive back into the pile, a chance for refreshment denied to the infant boys and the girls in the other playground. When I was playing there out of school hours I loved to pump some water and put my mouth to the cold stream that ran from the metal spout.

The field, with its good grazing, gnarled hawthorn by our gate, large old ash tree and younger oaks, and horse chestnut tree among others overlooking the road, sloped to a marsh through which the Ouse Gill Beck ran its course towards Kirby Hall. Summer sunshine and evening light played over a shallow pool, perfect for skimming flat pebbles, where the dammed-up beck widened before narrowing again near the fish-pond bridge. There a cutting gave access to water-carts – horse-drawn metal tanks on wheels, the farmers' means of replenishing the troughs in their fields. The beck is now confined to its channel and has become choked with reeds, but beyond the bridge it still flows through Kirby Hall Park to where, near Nun Monkton, it joins the River Ure, which then, unusually, becomes the Ouse.

Home, then, was the stone-built school house. The back door opened directly into the scullery, the pump and sink on the right, and a corner space for the wash-tub. This held the rubbing-board, various cloths, and the posser with its perforated copper head and wooden handle, which I have kept as a memento. My mother didn't use the wash-tub; even then a weekly laundry service from Boroughbridge collected bedding, tablecloths and my father's white starched collars. The pump provided rain-water from the school and house roofs, stored in a tank under the playground near the kitchen window. In a very dry summer it produced little more than moss and dirty drainings; in severe winter weather when the water froze, the pump yielded nothing and my mother would melt snow to boil handkerchiefs in a pan on the living room fire. Outside these rare extremes, there was ample for our needs and the water was soft and made good lather, but I knew only to drink water from the pump in the school yard. That never failed, but was so limy that it turned soap to thick, floating curds.

The marble-topped table by the window served for food preparation and, with a cushion, a seat for washing dirty feet in the sink. Its shallow drawer contained my father's cut-throat razors, a styptic pencil and alum block for cuts, talcum powder, toothpaste and toothbrushes, bread knife, carving knife and fork, vegetable knives and tin opener. The large, rectangular bread-board, which I still use occasionally for rolling pastry, stood at one end; a small old mirror hung on the wall to the left of the window; my potty was kept in a cupboard integral to the table. In front of the opposite wall was the three-burner paraffin stove, with a removable double oven standing over two burners. A home-made table stood by the door to the living room, near the roller towel.

Hot water? Yes, there was a small, lidded boiler, about a gallon in capacity. It was built into the range at the left side of the living room fireplace and on the right was an oven which neither my mother nor the previous headmaster's wife had been able to cajole beyond the temperature required for airing clothes. This large room was the centre of daytime family activities. The sewing machine stood by the window, with my mother's bookcase to its right, books in the glass-fronted cabinet, tablecloths and cutlery in one drawer, my small toys and games in another, the best crockery in the cupboard below and a row of shoes underneath. A wall clock hung above the deal-topped, all-purpose table, with its two spare leaves underneath and a chenille cover; a couple of hair-seated dining chairs were tucked under it. The small grate itself was set into the range as a whole, with its high mantelpiece, but it was backed by a huge shelf which would take half-burned coal for re-using, or empty food tins which had been put in the fire to sterilize them and were on their way to the refuse box. A 'tidy Betty' hid the falling ashes; an enamelled tin hearth-plate with a tile pattern covered the bare stone floor in front of the hearth and made a warm hiding place for nocturnal silverfish. When they became too obtrusive they were killed by the overnight use of Keatings' powder under the hearth-plate, and my mother swept them up as part of the morning routine of cleaning out the ashes and tidying the hearth. The whole fireside was surrounded by a large fireguard, drawn up to which was a rocking-chair with its back to the window.

Another bookcase, containing my father's gardening-books, encyclopaedias, *Mrs Beeton's Household Management* and a few classical novels, stood on a chest of drawers, which held all our underwear, spare sheets and a small drawer each for my parents' personal things. My mother's contained neatly folded pinafores and handkerchiefs, dust caps, hair brush, comb, purse and chocolate; my father's, string, two golf balls, a fez with a tassel, screw-drivers, the odd few nails, chalk, handkerchiefs, a drill whistle, two pen-knives, rubbers and pencil stubs, a spare pair of braces and other items in transit. Add a round, cloth-covered 'tufty' for a child to sit on, blazing fire in winter and a small one in summer to heat the water, the kettle or the irons, to make toast, or cook kippers or steak in a grid-iron, or simply to dispel the damp and chill of a sunless room, and you have all the makings of family life.

There were visitors and other residents too, the generations of mice that made their way through the crumbling mortar between the thick walls and stone floor, and popped out of their small holes in the skirting board behind the chest of drawers. Sometimes one would creep out from under it when we were sitting quietly by the fire and scuttle back when we moved. If they were sufficiently imprudent to be seen, or left droppings overnight and tooth marks in the cheese or turnips, my father would set traps baited with cheese at bedtime. I felt sad to see the broken-necked victims in the morning; I was quite fond of the mice.

Off the scullery was the 'wet' pantry, cold and dank, smelling of peeling whitewash and damp walls, with its stone table to keep food cool, mesh meat safes to keep off the flies, bucket of drinking water on the floor, jugs on hooks on the shelves, cooking utensils, everyday crockery. The 'dry' pantry backed onto the kitchen fireplace and held biscuits, dried peas and lentils, rice, sago and barley kernels, tins of food, Dinneford's Magnesia, California Syrup of Figs, Eno's Fruit Salts and the liquid paraffin my father took to ease his indigestion. Rarely used items were stored on the higher shelves. The pram and a box of toys occupied most of the floor. It was a warm place to play in, where I could build with bricks, float camphor-guided ducks on a bowl of water, or stroke the velvet cheeks of Peter, admire Marjorie Betty's closing eyelids with their real lashes, and finger the bone rings in Topsy's ears and around her dress.

Relaxed, companionable evenings were spent in the front room. There were easy chairs on either side of the fireplace, a drop-end settee facing it, a piano, a sideboard with lustres reflecting light from the elegant paraffin lamp hanging from a hook in the ceiling, a piano with a round piano-stool, and several leather-seated upright chairs. My father's desk and antiques cabinet stood to the left of the fireplace, the wireless stood on a small cupboard next to the sideboard and the whole room was presided over by the grandfather clock, ticking away the minutes until seven o'clock, bedtime. This was the stage on which I performed as the fairy queen or the head nurse, with my mother as sole audience, knitting or sewing. It was a room for pleasurable activity, such as eating lavishly buttered and salted potatoes, baked in the ashes under the grate and tangy from their blackened skins, or brooding over every juicy seed of a pomegranate before spitting the remnants into a saucer, or, if one's aim was good, into the fire. Before I went to bed, my dad would join us to eat a potato or share an apple, cutting it into metallic-tasting slices with his penknife. This was an all-purpose tool, but a wipe on his trousers would make it fit to serve as a fruit knife.

When morning sunlight caught the lustres, sending rainbows dancing on the walls, and brightened patches of carpet, and dust motes danced in the beams as my mother dusted the furniture and plumped cushions, the room was warmed by a different magic. I was allowed to climb onto the settee and hold the ornaments from the piano top. I would carefully cuddle the two china dogs, admire the folds of the woman's clothing and the hat of the young man going to sea or to seek his fortune, with his bundle and stick at his feet, who was fingering the sharpness at the top of the background tree. Next came two Toby jugs, one wide, cracked and crazed and light in weight, the other heavy, shiny, immaculate in porcelain, with tricorn hat and a black spot on Toby's cheek; I didn't handle the carefully repaired porcelain candlestick with its mother and child figures, and I wasn't interested in the less attractive barometer, with its dull, dark wood frame, glass-covered brass pointers, numbers and words which eventually gained meaning. The plush, grey fabric of the settee prickled bare thighs; exploring little fingers loved to trace the pattern and eventually learned to operate the metal catch to lower the drop end.

Some of my earliest memories were of my parents making cane chairs, tables and trays there, bending and weaving the soaked cane, and later my mother making lifelike paper flowers from Dennison's crepe paper and preparing templates for her demonstrations to the Women's Institute. I was trusted to stretch strips of paper and twist them round thin canes for the stems. The carpet had a square pattern suitable for games of marbles. My mother and I played, or I would take the part of both players and try to manipulate the winner. As I grew older, I would lie on the floor in front of the fire and read, and eventually the hearth rug was the place for French homework and history revision. The floor was always a better source of inspiration than a desk or table.

Upstairs were three bedrooms. In the cot beside my parents' bed, I would wake and clamour, 'I want to come into your bed.' When ignored while they pretended to be still asleep, this became a repetitive, rhythmical 't'your bed', 'chor bed', accompanied by bouncing until I won the contest. I never got tired of chanting, because I loved the sound of the words and the rhythm of jumping, and I will admit to a certain determination to win. When I had my own room I would creep into my parents' bed to make sure they were awake, and lie there with my mother for word games and nursery rhymes after my father had gone downstairs to light the fire, boil a kettle to make a pot of tea, warm milk for me on the kitchen stove, and enjoy his first cigarette of the day.

In the dark of winter, the domain above the first landing and bend in the stairs was a place of terror. Somewhere along the upstairs corridor, or in the spare room, lurked the bogey man whose name I have tried for years to remember. He could be kept at bay by the light of a paraffin lamp, but I was not allowed to carry one. I would dash upstairs in the dark, heart racing, to fetch something from the bedroom by the glimmer of window light from the night sky only if my dad would stand at the bottom of the stairs and sing, 'Cock-a-doodle, cock-a-doodle, I'm the cock of the north,' until I came safely back to the staircase and scampered down. By daylight, the staircase was a source of inventive play, a challenge to discover how many different ways I could devise of coming down: stretch out and slide as if I were a toboggan; sit on each step and bump down to the next; slide on my tummy propelling myself by pushing off the edges of the steps; jump down two at a time, carefully hanging on to the banister; jump off the last one, then two, then three. I didn't exactly perform these feats with careless abandon; even the ultimate, daring escapade of sliding down the banister was taken slowly, with due caution, and rather quietly to avoid attracting attention.

At night, in winter, when I was very young, the bedroom was haunted by shadows cast by the paraffin lamp or the Valor Perfection heater, which had a patterned top and sides. The dancers on the walls shimmered with the movement of the blue flame; the dark wedge on the ceiling varied in shape according to how far the door had been left open, and was capable of 'getting' me in spite of the high bars of the cot. I didn't visualize what that meant, but the very idea set my stomach trembling. I decreed that they could all be kept in their place by burying my head in the bedclothes out of their sight, singing a tuneless song and cuddling Ted, my teddy-bear and constant companion. If I had a cold, he had eucalyptus oil on his nose; if we went out in the pram, he went, too; if my mother was packing for a visit to Castleford, I always reminded her that, 'we musn't terget about Ted'. As a mark of affection I would 'smigs' him – rub noses, a privilege I extended to none other. My mother gave Ted a new nose in black wool whenever the previous one was smigsed bare.

Outside the house, down two jumpable steps, was our back yard, separated from the school playground by a concealing wall and tall gate. To the right, set into an even higher wall, was the garden gate, itself high and wide. At right angles, by the coal-place wall, stood two dustbins, one for fine ashes to be rolled into the garden path, the other for soot to be put round the vegetables to keep off pests. When I was big enough, I liked to lift and clatter the lid of the ash bin, but the acrid, powdery black soot puffed out as the air stirred it when the other lid was lifted.

Round the corner was the door to the coal-place, its contents replaced regularly by the Atkinsons, their faces sweaty and shiny, black with dust, humping coal on their backs in open hessian bags filled at the gate from their lorry and held by 'ears' formed with tight string, then, with a quick body turn, emptied in a rattling cascade and a cloud of dust; grimy hands held out for coins, broken black fingernails. The coal-place also held dry kindling – thick and thin dead twigs of oak, ash, hawthorn and whatever the wind provided, collected by my mother and me in fields and lanes, broken to a convenient size and neatly aligned in boxes, the only way, I was told, to ensure that the boxes held as much as possible and the sticks were easy to take out. They were carefully matched for size and thickness and the ease with which they fitted alongside each other, a nice little job for me. A half-rusty shovel, its wooden handle smoothed and grimed by daily use, loose on its slack nail, scraped the floor as the coal was scooped up to clatter into metal buckets, larger pieces and slack carefully mixed so that nothing was wasted. Coal was a joy to brood over: shiny, smooth surfaces, slaty, with grey streaks, fern patterns; dirty fingers wiped down a dress; black shoe prints.

Life in the back yard centred on the wash kitchen, a combined workshop and tool store, for me an adventure playground. The square, brick-built stove filled one corner, with its copper set-pot and wooden lid, deep, ashy fireplace underneath, and chimney going out through the roof. My mother never used it to heat water for washing, but made do with the fireside boiler. She carried bowlfuls of squeezed and folded clothes to the wringer near the wash kitchen door, removed the dust cover and turned the green-painted, metal wheel to operate the thick wooden rollers as she fed the washing between them. The cloudy water trickled and spread down a wooden tray and dribbled through a hole to splash and tinkle into a bucket underneath. I could entertain myself with the creaking wringer by swinging the handle from side to side, pushing it high and watching it drop back, a quick pendulum, then stillness. I was careful not to touch the claggy, blackened grease that eased the turning of the wheel.

Every Friday night my father lit the fire under the set-pot to heat water for the tin bath, which he brought from its hook in the wash kitchen to stand in front of the kitchen fire. In memory it is always winter, and bathing a tense experience by lamp-light: water too hot, draughts too cold, unpleasant soaping a slippery invasion of my private space; screams if my dad came into the room, because he would see my toes; wonder at my two 'spotties' and an absolute embargo on touching my 'hole', even if it did have fluff in it. With the bath pushed aside, it was a joy at last to sit, safe inside a nightie on a comforting knee in front of the fire, and welcome then to have my toes warmed by my mother's hand, while I gazed into the fire, was fascinated by the crackling log, the dancing yellow flames, the small blue ones licking around the black coal or hovering over the red embers. 'Waaarm her toe-toes, her preeety little toe-toes', and then I admired my small toes, and giggled and permitted the piggies to go to market, giggling when the little one 'cried *wee wee wee* – all the way home!' – all the way to my arm-pit.

The wash kitchen was my father's territory into which my mother strayed occasionally when necessary. The thick-topped workbench dominated the left-hand side, scarred, darkened oak, fissures lightened by a filling of fine sawdust, the shelf underneath filled with plywood, new wood, bits of old wood, skeins of thin cane, and bases and frames for making cane trays and furniture. When the canework hobby ended, the shelf was filled with stackable wooden fruit boxes, new and old, ready for seedlings or sprouting potatoes, or soil-encrusted, waiting for repair. Alice-like, I grew and could see onto the top. The vice, like the wringer, became controllable: turn the grimy wooden handle to make the block ride on its thick wooden screw, narrow or wide; put something into it and try to hold it straight and steady while I turned the handle; frustration when it slipped, try again. Tools were always around: boat-shaped wooden planes with sharp blades, knobbly files to test tender fingers; and saws, oh, yes; saws with big, jagged teeth or fine teeth filled with dust remnants, short saws, long saws, bendy saws, oily saws, stiff saws; warm wooden handles with peeling varnish, cold blades, their teeth bright with recent use or reddened with rust, orangey-red rust that could be rubbed onto fingers; look how it fills the creases, smoothes the tips.

Under the window stood a chest of drawers containing scratched and grimy tobacco tins and catarrh-pastille tins rattling with nails and screws, screwdrivers and chisels, sticks of solder, the soldering-iron, wire and string and innumerable oddments – just the right thing for the job in hand. My favourite plaything was a drill. Fascinated, I turned the handle and watched the oiled cogs of its red disk engage with the smaller ones, turning faster and faster, vibrating and growling. I wasn't interested in the pack of bits unless my dad was using the tool. Then I followed its wobbling progress as the bit slowly opened a hole in the marked spot, the knobbly sound gradually smoothing, the grindings gathering in the metal grooves and the plop as it suddenly broke through and the point pierced the protective block underneath. The top of the chest held small garden tools, the stinking glue-pot, and enough happy clutter to stimulate any handyman to heights of optimistic inventiveness. A barrel in the corner by the wringer was stuffed with garden canes, longer tools and brushes, and a set of golf clubs, unused throughout my childhood – just there, until the irons tarnished, the wooden ones crumbled in worm holes and the leather grips cracked and hardened.

The whole space smelt of things about to be done. It was waiting for the echo of hammer on nail, plane cutting off tendrils of resinous shavings and smoothing dark roughness to golden-grained beauty, woody scents driving away the dusty staleness rising from the floor; the clatter of a stout box, inverted as a saw-horse. Start at the other side. Sandpaper the cut end smooth; time for a cigarette and a cup of tea. What joy then, quietly alone, to finger the grainy sawdust. Such beauty, to be dirtied by sweeping, put in a bucket for the compost heap; curled shavings, soon to be shovelled up and put aside for kindling; I wanted to cherish them for ever and run my fingers over the curves of the thin wood, delight in the near-transparent line of the grain, feel the prickly sharp end.

The mending of a bucket, a watering can, the crack where the handle was leaving a pan, was an event. My dad plunged the soldering-iron into the kitchen fire and put out the tin of soft, pale-brown, greasy flux and a stick of solder. We stood back while he took the red-hot iron out of the fire and rushed through the kitchen, trailing heat and sulphurous smoke, out to the wash kitchen. I dashed after him to watch, while he dipped the iron into the flux, which smoked and sizzled, then rubbed the prepared iron over the patch to be mended and held it against the stick of soft solder, so that it melted in shiny drops onto the hole. With the hot iron, dipped again in flux, he rubbed and shaped the solder to a smooth repair and let everything cool.

Beside the wash kitchen, sharing its roof, was an L-shaped space containing the 'closet'. The larger, dark area behind it was the wood store. The narrow part held the bicycles and a forty-gallon drum of paraffin with its pump and spout, and the fishing tackle, balanced on long, stout nails on the wall. I didn't go round the back to the wood pile; the dark corners were black with ancient cobwebs, and the inhabitants of the most recent lived their lives there safe from human interference. In spring, the swallows returned to their nests on the beams and raised their brood of young, which gathered on the clothes line, at first to try their wings and delight us with their efforts to fly, later in preparation for migration. This gathering filled me with sadness and longing.

The enclosed 'closet' had a door to separate it from the narrow passage and confine the smell. It was lime-washed and, at the back, was a wooden bench with a single hole and enough space for neat pieces of newspaper. Its hinged front hid the two-handled rectangular zinc container, emptied weekly on Saturdays by the caretaker, along with those the children used. The throat-catching, pungent stench wafted out as the door was opened, and disinfectant did little to disguise it. As a young child I wasn't allowed to use the place, and I sympathize with my mother's embarrassment and distaste when compelled to accept this primitive aspect of village life. I tried to ignore the whole corner, with its unseen lovers of the dark, its narrow, cluttered passage, and the 'closet'.

Outside the garden gate, a border, a path and a sloping lawn fronted the house, bisected by the steps and stone path that led from the road to the front door. The whole frontage was bounded by spiked iron railings, with a matching front gate. The house reflected its church-school origin, arched windows with tiny panes, heavy, arched door, with a ring-operated sneck and a bell-pull that rang a tongued brass bell dangling from a flexible metal holder in the hall.

The garden continued along the side of the house and schoolrooms and round the outside of the infants' classroom to join the girls' playground. Another stretch of garden lay between that playground and the field. All this was my home ground, particularly after school hours; I explored it all, grew beyond it, but it remains a precious memory, a sanctuary of the heart.

House and garden, school and field, the centre of my world, set in the village street, where people passed by, caught up in the routine of week and season. Figures in a landscape, characters in a drama played out in a child's mind, they came and went, walked and worked, led horses and carts, brought round and sold their goods, gossiped in doorways, scrubbed steps, sat quietly in the afternoon sun, strolled on summer evenings, hunched against autumn wind and rain, plodded through snow. A few I knew well, and these we shall meet as they come back briefly from the world they lived in, remote and unattainable after almost four decades of change.

We were in the village, but not of the village, and the school house was a small, enclosed world, the more so because there were no children of my age at that end of the village. My parents, for reasons that seemed good to them at the time, withdrew from the Wesleyan Chapel and any participation in village affairs that might have made them appear to be taking sides in controversy. It suited my father to live his own quiet life outside working hours and my mother was obsessed with privacy: her self-image as the schoolmaster's wife, a cut above the village people, insulated both her and me, with few exceptions, from warm and friendly relationships. My childhood memories are of a village as remote as an old photograph, where things looked different, smelled different, were done differently and with a simplicity that had to change.

Perhaps now is the time for first impressions. Some memories survive from my first year, but time ripples through these early years, bringing few clear-cut recollections of whether I was two, three, four, or all of these; there was continuity and change. This was the time when I was at home with Mommy, before I crossed the boys' yard, passed through the gate and beyond the wall, into the playground shared by the girls and infants, and so to school.

CHAPTER II

Echoes of infancy and early childhood

Experience and memory began in the living room, cushioned in a deep, dark-blue pram, between the sewing machine, the bookcase, the table and the rocking-chair, the bright window to the right. Just a snatched image: eyes open to a hazy, looming, brownish shape on the left, a familiarity, curiosity, a 'surely I remember ...' feeling without words, and the image fades. No cot, no other place, the pram the centre of waking life, apart from arms, the rocking-chair. Language in a simple form, there from the beginning; things heard, when? Before birth? Who can be sure? But this I know; these are memories I have always lived with. Language, echoing in sounds, rhythms, repeated words, listened to in my mind. My father's arms, the rocking-chair, rocking, gently rocking; a voice: '...I get the tea-tin'; the tea-tin, tea-tin, rock, rock, the tea-tin, tea-tin; red, gold edge of the lid shining in the window light, high on the end of the mantelpiece above the rocking chair. My mother reaches up, light-coloured, and the tin moves; tea-tin, tea-tin, bouncing, lingering, rocking sound. I was told later that my eyes would follow the tea-tin when I was around three or four months old. Daddy singing,

> Wo, ti wo, ti wum pum pum,
> Wo, ti wo, ti wum pum pum,
> And when si dipersi doo,
> O den si dipsi dee,
> And si dipsi dopsi disi dosi
> Dum pum pum.

'Sing "wo ti wo", Daddy,' a memory of a request. When did I say it aloud? How old was I when he stopped rocking me and singing it? I don't know, but I can hear my voice asking repeatedly for the song associated only with Daddy and the rocking chair.

In Mommy's arms in the kitchen; Daddy shaving in front of the mirror, pulling his face into shapes, thick lather yielding to a shiny, black-handled cut-throat razor previously sharpened on the leather strop that hung from a hook near the roller towel. 'A dada, a dada', contemplative, defining.

Sudden excitement: 'She said it! She said "Dada". She knows, you know.'

In my mind, indignation: 'Of course I know; I've been saying it for a long time.'

A game of passing the parcel, with me as the parcel, insecure, not liking this at all: Mommy by the fireguard, Daddy in the rocking chair:

'I don't want you, *go* to your Daddy!'

'I don't want you, *go* to your Mommy!'

They'd have been horrified to think that I understood and have remembered for all these years.

I'm sitting in the pram, bouncing in my frustrating harness. I chew the end of the leather strap, clamping gums, myum, myum, tasty, slimy now, smooth side, hairy rough side, fierce leather taste. Twist, explore the button-hole fasteners at the side of the pram; cold metal, roundness; look, it dents my fingertips. Pull the leather tab; it bends and stays fixed. Bounce, whimper, try to pull myself up, wriggle. Yes, I can turn a little in the restraint, hard on shoulders and tummy, collapse in frustration; whimper, bounce. The pram rocks and the springs creak. That's interesting. Listen to myself myuming in time to the creak and bounce. How did I manage to chew the central part of the leatherette-covered edge of the pram hood down to the bare metal? I remember the taste, and the evidence lasted as long as the pram.

Jumbo and Dora, my first rubber pram toys; Jumbo has a squeak, a metal-rimmed hole under his tummy. Squeeze him and he squeaks – amusing, predictable. Make me giggle by squeaking Jumbo in front of my face and rubbing my nose with his trunk. I can do it myself, slowly. I feel the cold air rush out with a rubber smell as he squeaks; finger over the hole, he stays fat, no squeak. Chew his trunk, his foot; rub it across gums, fiercely; hurty, but satisfying. Wet trunk, dribble. I see him now as he lay in my drawer over the years. When did the lines on his trunk begin to crumble as the rubber hardened? When did I finally pull the end off? Chew Dora's rubber foot, cool dribble on hot gums. Rub it along and listen to the squeak of wet rubber on toothless gums. I can make it happen. Do it again. She lay for years in the same drawer in a small, blue and white knitted dress, with her nibbled, tooth-marked feet, and I remember picking fragments of rubber from my slimy tongue and the taste and smell of wet wool.

There were other pram toys, particularly Rob Roy, with his head and shoulders of white pot, painted black hair and eyes, rosy cheeks and tiny mouth. His body, arms and legs were moulded from pink fabric stuffed with finely shredded wood shavings and sawdust and stitched at the joints. His legs from the knees down were white pot with painted black boots. He had some clothes, but he didn't often wear them because I enjoyed poking the glue at the joint where his head was fastened onto his body. Eventually, the fabric gave way, his head and shoulders wobbled and he shed prickly stuffing – interesting.

Thirteen months old and not yet able to walk; standing by the fireguard, warmth on my face, clinging on with one hand, feeling the warm metal denting my flesh; a noise by the chest of drawers; two huge figures with a smaller one between them; panic; stumble against the trufty; can't get to Mommy's knee quickly. 'It's all right, darling; it's only Auntie Gertie and Uncle Reub and Cousin Kenneth.' I relax; I know who they are. I realize now that this must have been the October half-term holiday and that they had previously visited us with Grandma and the uncles during Ken's summer holiday. Gert died three weeks later of a cerebral haemorrhage, aged forty-two. My mother never overcame the bitterness she felt on losing her adored older sister, particularly since Reub married again a year later. For me it meant that my cousin, who became like an older brother, spent large parts of his school holidays with us until he went to college, and even then he remained a frequent visitor in his college blazer. He brought fun and laughter and, later, companionship into my childhood in a way nobody else did, from the days when he sat me on his knee, teased me about the way I said my name and christened me 'Mut', and I made appallingly over-kneaded, over-baked, small 'mut-loaves' for him which he dutifully ate with a smile of exaggerated pleasure, to the times when I watched as he carved the *Good Ship Mary Ann* out of wood and knotted her rigging, or tried to explain the mysteries of magnetos when he was building a wireless set. Years later we walked in the darkness of the country lanes and he showed me some of the constellations in the brilliant night sky and shared his scepticism about the existence of God; a comfortable bond of unchanging affection remained until he died.

Now I'm sitting on my mother's knee and pressing my chin, as usual into the warm dent in the leatherette top of the rocking chair made by the pressure of working my lower jaw up and down. But I'm not enjoying the warm hollow and smell of leatherette, I am gazing at the light from the window; the dent is wet and tacky; I'm crying. I'm irritated by my mother's rubbing of my back and singing her usual comfort song, 'nassy ol' pain in little tummy tum tum'. I know I haven't got tummy-ache. I don't have words for the cause of my distress, but it isn't that, and I cry harder because she doesn't understand.

I'm older, and we're rocking and singing nursery rhymes in the afternoon, sending all the characters down Youjar (short for Youjarkerpiv):

There's little Bo-Peep down Youjar,
Down Youjar, so they say.
Little Bo-Peep lost her sheep
Down Youjar way.
Then hey, boys, stay, boys,
Don't go away;
There's sure to be a little bit of fun today,
'Cos a cushy-cow's coming,
A cushy-cow's coming,
Coming all the way from Youjar.

We send little Miss Muffet and little Jack Horner, down Youjar, and then little Boy Blue.

'No, Mommy, it's not right.'

'Yes, it is.'

She sings, 'Little Boy Blue, come blow up your horn' and it fits the tune. It does fit the tune, but it doesn't rhyme. I know it's wrong, but I can't explain why. I don't have the vocabulary to argue; resentfully, I let it go. As usual, I wake up on the settee in the front room with no memory of how I got there.

It's a dull, slow afternoon and it's raining. I'm tired of being indoors and I'm 'wittering' because I want to play in the yard. She sings:

Rain, rain, go away,

Come again another day,

Little girlies want to play,

Rain, rain, rain.

I go to the door again and look out, but it's still raining. So much for magic!

My early impressions of the exciting world outside the cot and pram were from a squatter's view, close to the ground, smells and textures intensified, the scents, the warmth and cold rising, the sharp focus on inanimate objects, on moving, growing things. Lino, carpet, ashy paths, grass and soil were the first playgrounds in which I squatted.

The drab, brown lino with its smooth surface and chevron pattern smelt of plastic and coarse fibre backing. The corners curled and could be poked up to release the smell of damp from its stained underside and the floor, with possibly a dusty bit of cobweb and a scuttle of spider. The large, traditional rag rug, a mixture of coloured, variously shaped patches, which partly covered the carpet in front of the living room fire, was made from old clothes. It had seen several years of use; the central patches were already becoming worn, while others still retained their ragged edges. It was satisfying to pull bits of cut thread from the longer ones and trace the strips back to the sackcloth, where ashy dust collected, or finger a shiny patch, black from an old spill.

Away from that squatter's heaven, the back yard and wash kitchen, my favourite squatting-place was the 'slope', the gravel area beyond the playground, leading to the school gate. The pebbles, probably brought from the local gravel pit, but tumbled by ancient seas before the last Ice Age, lay in their compacted sandy bed, trodden in by children's feet as they walked up to the playground in small groups at the beginning of the day, and dashed to the gate, boys' hob-nailed boots skittering down the slope in a near slide, on the way home. Channels eroded by rain-water, in which bigger pebbles lay in strange patterns like boulders in a stream, snaked down to the gate. In these pre-school years, and for some years afterwards, I squatted to enjoy holding the dark ones in my hand, wiping off the dust and watching their colour deepen in response to my sweaty warmth. Best of all were the 'lucky stones'; I was utterly happy looking for lucky stones, the crystalline quartz rounded to tiny perfection or with small flaws ingrained with sand, and I would seek out the perfect ones, pure white, or streaked with colour. A very few favoured specimens were kept for years among my treasures, but I took most of them into the house to show my mother and then put them back. It never struck me that I might be seeing the same ones over and over again; the experience was always an exploration.

I didn't spend much time with toys unless I had to stay indoors. Squatting fed my love of contemplation, my deep longing, even then, to be close to the earth. I was enchanted by the variety, fascinated by long, slow tracing of patterns in nature, in touch with moving, growing, tender, emerging life rather than objects made by human ingenuity. Soil, shining smooth and moist from the spade, or sun-dried and fissured, soft or crumbly, was full of sinuous, glistening creatures that birds love, climbing mountains, snaking through valleys, avoiding dangerous precipices or, after struggling in vain to conquer an obstacle, taking the easy way round it. Worm-holes pitted the lawn, with conical piles of fine grains beside them, and worms shone in the newly turned earth when my father was digging: small red ones, big lug-worms from the manure heap dug out as fishing bait, ribbed, with saddles round them, and ordinary, greyish-pink worms with small saddles, struggling away from the light. I would hold the big ones by one end and watch them wriggle, before releasing them to flop heavily onto the soil, or let the smaller ones perform their uneasy acrobatics in the warm hollow of my hand.

Lawns were wet with a haze of dew in which footprints made a dark trail as the cold dampness soaked sandals and feet; or dry and parched, smelling of dusty soil that crept grittily between the toes; or newly mown, smelling of cut grass and sprinkled with smatterings of clippings, the soil striped by the rake. They were a luxuriant mixture: grass spears, soft and tender, unlike those of the field and roadside which, coarse with hairs, scratchily resisted being stroked the wrong way; clover, fine-leaved, hugging the ground, flowering fresh and greenish white, or tingeing pink and browning as it faded, creeping with tough stems close to the soil among the grasses; self-heal, with furry blue flowers and rough little rounded leaves; pert daisies with pink-tinged white ray petals and yellow button centres; tough little plantains and persistent dandelions. The best of these, flowering brashly, were at the sides of the paths and in the borders, or stood erect, with fluffily perfect heads, waiting for a breeze. I enjoyed them all, long before I looked for four-leaved clovers, which were quite common in the front lawn and on the verges outside, or made daisy-chains and pulled off the white petals, saying, 'He loves me, he loves me not,' or measured time by blowing the dandelion clocks. I was attracted to small flowers in the borders. Before I knew their names I squatted over the rings of annuals through their brief seasons: godetia, with colourful caps and stiff seed pods; 'love-in-a-mist', the delicate nigella, with finely cut, hazy leaves and squeezable pods; ursinia, with deep yellow flowers and button seed heads bursting with little parachutes; clarkia, taller, soft in shades of pink, with hard pods, resisting nails probing them to test their ripeness and admire the rows of seeds within. I loved the smell of bruised eschscholtzia leaves and the pixie caps of their opening flowers. These could be lifted gently, releasing the crumpled petals to spread unspoilt in the sunshine. But my particular affection was for the pansies lining the border. My mother used to sing, 'All those little pansy faces, growing in the garden there,' and my dad allowed me to pick as many as I wished, because 'the more they're picked, the better they flower'. I gave them personalities and picked the friendliest ones. Another self-appointed task was to pop fuchsia heads to help them into flower, a habit that started young. I find the prospect of a satisfying 'pop' from a fully developed fuchsia bud hard to resist even now.

It was still natural to squat when I had grown well beyond choosing pebbles and looking at my face in a pool, distorted by a shiver of wind or the first drops of rain. I did not   quickly abandon the skill of floating hawthorn-petal boats and bits of grass on pools of rainwater; it lasted long into the time of swinging, and pelting down the girls' yard on my scooter and poking cow-claps with a stick to see if they were ripe or if the cows had worms. Only I knew of the small space at the base of the old ash tree in Jacksons' field where, as a twelve-year-old, I squatted furtively with racing heart to hide the red lip salve bought secretly in Knaresborough Woolworths. Only I knew that you could push such treasures out of sight beyond the dry soil, safely round a corner into the hollow where thick bark became root.

Whenever the weather was fine, my mother and I went for a walk. At first it was a pram-ride in my deep, dark-blue pram. As I got older, the middle cushion could be removed and I sat with my feet in the well. On one memorable occasion I was encouraged to toddle along holding the bars which extended under the pram, feeling proud of myself, if insecure. Quite often, Miss Harrison went with us. She lodged next door and was 'lady's companion' to wealthy Miss Thompson, who lived in Kirkholme, near the church. She was probably in her late forties, jolly and smiling, and was the nearest my mother had to a friend in those early years. I never knew why she left the village or where she went, but I believe she was ill. We never heard from her, which tells its own story. When we turned down Boat Lane we looked across the low hedges of the corner field and played, *"I can see School House!" "So can I!"* Well, they played and I understood and giggled.

Later, when I was too old for the pram, my mother regularly took me down the road as far as the fish-pond bridge, or to the corner by Little Ouseburn church. This ritual followed the first job of the morning, cleaning out the ashes, sweeping the hearth, washing the hearth-plate. I had a drink of juice, freshly squeezed from an orange, used the potty whether I wanted to or not – a source of vocal objection and stamping – and had my face and hands rubbed with an unpleasant, wet flannel, and my arms pushed into my coat, which was then fastened and pulled down smartly. We usually took 'croc', who was really a snake, but had been defined as a crocodile; perhaps snakes had too strong an association with Satan. He was made from shiny, brightly-painted wooden beads threaded onto soft, red string, with a loop on the end to slip over my wrist. His head was a shaped bead which held the biggest knot in his open mouth. I used to pull him along behind me, and eventually the beads became scarred and flattened on the underside and the paint less bright. One day we returned home to discover that he had lost his tail, a long, narrow bead. We went back, but couldn't find it, so my dad made him another from a piece of drilled and whittled wood, but it wasn't smooth, and the dull red water-colour was no substitute for the hard red bead of the tail he'd lost. Fickle as I was, my affection waned.

My memories of those walks are mostly of early summer, the air scented warmly by the profusion of wild roses rambling over the hedge between the field and the track to the stream, near the bridge. I would walk on the raised stone pathway on either side of the bridge and be lifted up to look over the parapet at the bulrushes on the Kirby Hall side and towards the school on the other. Timing was obviously important, because a sudden eruption of sound would signify playtime, and later, on the way home, a hand-bell would be heard ringing its signal to form lines and go indoors again.

One thing I dreaded was that we might have to pass Percy Cuthbert, who was responsible for sweeping the village street and footpath, cutting the grass verges which ran the whole length of the village and beyond, clearing the gutters and keeping down the coarsest weeds. His tools were a wheel-barrow, a stiff-bristled sweeping-brush, a spade, a shovel, a scythe, and a sickle with a short, curved blade. The last of these terrified me, all the more because he was thick-set and taciturn, with ruddy complexion and brown, hairy arms. He wore a flannel shirt, corduroy trousers, held up by braces and a leather belt and tied at the ankles with 'billy band' (binder twine), and thick, hob-nailed boots. His 'good morning' was a grunt, unaccompanied by a smile. I was convinced, having by this time met some of the ogres pictured in story-books, that he intended to cut off my head with the sickle. If I saw him using it, I averted my face and covered my eyes with my hands as we walked past; I never uttered a word when occasionally he extended his grunt to a greeting or a brief conversation. When I was four, all this changed. For my fourth birthday we got a miniature Yorkshire terrier puppy called Tusie, and I held her lead proudly when we went for our walk. Percy was trimming the bank below Starra Cottage with the dreaded sickle:

'That's a nice little dog. Can I 'ave your dog?'

'*No*, you may *not* have the dog. It's *my* dog.'

Astonishment and amusement on the part of Percy and my mother, much to my indignation!

He was one of the village characters, and a pleasanter man than my childish imagination would allow. Road-sweeping is thirsty work, and his reputation was that, in the *Three Horse Shoes* at dinner-time, the first pint went down in one long swallow and the second made him sociable. The Cuthberts lived in one of the group of houses near the *Bay Horse*, and Percy's wife, well spoken and smartly dressed, was always ready to chat when we met her in the street. When I was about twelve they adopted an orphaned niece, Dorothy, a friendly girl. I pitied her, without any justification, I'm sure, but my early fear lingered.

Tusie made a big difference to my last pre-school months. I had always been attracted to cats and dogs and rather too willing to approach any that were passing. She arrived one afternoon in a small, lidded wicker basket. My father and Ken had been to Harrogate in Ken's first car to collect her. The basket was put onto the living-room table and she emerged, a blackish ball of fluff with a brown head and legs. At first I didn't know what she was. 'Is it real? Is it a chicken?' I knew it wasn't a chicken, but it didn't look much like my idea of either a dog or a new toy. My dad put her down on the floor and she tottered onto the lino, squatted, and did a huge pool. I was delighted. 'It's real; it's done poosie!' Throughout her puppyhood we were inseparable companions. Wherever I danced about the house, she followed me; if I jumped onto and off the tufty, she did the same; whenever I ran in the school yard, she ran as well. I didn't mind brushing her, but regarded it as Mommy's job to wash her face and bottom and tie her topknot with a ribbon.

She soon learned that my dad took her out into the garden to do her business. He'd only to say, 'Where's my cap?' and she would run round in circles and dash for the back door. Her bed was a wooden box set on its side in front of the fireplace, with a blanket and cushion in it and another on top for a seat, the tufty being set to one side. Both cushions had covers made from squares knitted with wool from old jumpers. As a young puppy she weighed about half a pound, and only three pounds when fully grown. She was the smallest Yorkshire terrier I've ever seen. When awake, she was always eager, panting with excitement, her pink tongue hanging out and curling at the edges. She went everywhere with us, including to Scarborough on holiday. When I took her out on the lead along the sea-front, people would exclaim and comment. I made a point of telling them how old she was if they assumed she was a puppy. She died when I was fifteen and was buried in the rockery outside the front room window.

When I was about four and a half I made a very big mistake. I told my parents that I knew what the children did in the playground and I wanted to know what they did in school. It was mere curiosity on my part, but, to my horror and panic they took it seriously, So ended my familiar routine of reading with my mother, following the words in the stories about Meg and Martin and Minnie and Mopsa who went to the fair, and the kind little boy who helped his weary mother to turn the mangle on washing day, or sitting on her knee while she read me stories of Jack and the Beanstalk, Jack the Giant-killer, Hansel and Gretel and the sweet-stuff house, and nursery rhymes, nature stories and

Grimm's Fairy Tales. No more contented hours spent making cut-out patterns from coloured paper, floating cigarette-card transfers on water in the vain hope of mounting them successfully, sending my rows of dolls through Sandgate while I danced and sang. Of course, I didn't stop doing these things, but, for the first time, I experienced the insecurity of daily life amongst other children and the tensions of relating to them as the schoolmaster's daughter.

CHAPTER III

Village life: neighbours and shopkeepers

The view today from the windows of the school house, or front of the school as it is now, bears no resemblance to the way it was when we lived there. A tall, older house still stands a little way up from the school, close to the road behind its hedge. That, and a number of the surrounding cottages, had belonged formerly to Dr Pope who, in chronic ill health, had been looked after by a resident nurse, Miss Peach. His legacy to her was that the house should be her home for life, together with the income from the cottages, which would provide her with nearly the equivalent of a farm labourer's wage. She lived there alone, reclusively and with increasingly failing eyesight, throughout the years I lived in the village. I can't ever remember seeing her walking in the street, but she appeared quite frequently at the gate to look out, a dumpy, round-faced woman with a wispy, greying bun, thick glasses and high colour. To me she was frighteningly ancient; when I was old enough to go to the shops on errands I wanted to hurry past the house, averting my eyes in case she was at the window lifting the net curtain. Unlike the cottages, this house seemed alien, with its overbearing proximity to the road and shrouded windows. I realize now how little I saw of relationships among those who lived in Pope's cottages. Probably Miss Peach had a garden or yard behind the house, accessible to her kindly neighbours, who would fetch her water and help her in other ways, but I saw nothing of it. I suspect that she grew old there in genteel simplicity, always an outsider in the village as a whole.

The larger group of these cottages stood parallel to the road, and several more were situated up a short, roughly surfaced lane beyond Miss Peach's house. They all had substantial gardens in a field-sized plot behind the out-buildings and shared a pump in a large yard near the road. The biggest, a detached house with a large garden and orchard, was opposite the front gate of the school house. Today its entrance and part of the front garden form the road into the small modern estate which has replaced the lively community I knew. In my childhood the Parkers lived there with their grown-up family. Mr Parker was small and thin, with strongly lined, weather-beaten skin, a pipe between his sunken lips, and a smiling face. Mrs Parker was still beautiful, with a round maturity and a mass of wavy white hair gathered softly into a bun. They were sociable in retirement and could often be seen chatting to passers-by at the gate.

The eldest girl, Joyce, used to go out to work early, on her bicycle. Marjorie had a small business delivering newspapers round the village. They arrived by van from York early in the morning; the thick packet was thrown deftly into the drive. She always put a poster with headlines in a stand by the gate; some of them were printed on coloured paper and looked bright and eye-catching. When my mother had a phase of making fire-screens and magazine racks from painted wood and varnished paper beads, she begged these posters because they were colourful when cut into strips for the bead-making machine. Wallace Parker was about twenty-one when I first became aware of him. He came to live next door to us several years later when he married a much older woman, Kitty Walker. Later, he taught me to drive; later still, when I came home on Friday evenings from Huddersfield, he gave me lifts from York, where he worked collecting insurance premiums. He was a kindly tease, always good for a laugh, and was a friend and yarning-companion to my father, both of them having an equal love of leaning on a spade and smoking. I first remember him as keeper to 'Barrett's bloomin' elephant', but more of that in due course. Dick was a little younger, a handsome, dark-haired lad, and Eric, 'Baggy' Parker, was the youngest at about sixteen, cheerful and round-faced, always whistling. They were a lively, good-natured family, who whizzed about on bicycles, bells ringing in farewell to their mother, who would stand in the doorway to wave them off.

Eventually all married, the old couple died, and the cottage fell into disrepair, there being no interest in it from the younger generation of the Pope family and no money to keep it or the other cottages in good condition. During the war my father was permitted to use the garden, occupying energetic teenage evacuees and older local children by growing vegetables. The garden had a wealth of fruit, black, red and white currants, green and red gooseberries, raspberries, cherry rhubarb of a thickness I haven't seen since we left its offspring in Dunsforth, apples, pears, and a beautiful old tree of pin damsons, small, tangy, flavoursome fruit which made delicious jam and fruit pies.

A terrace of four cottages faced the road and the school. Each had a small front garden, an iron gate, its posts set into a large flag-stone, and a cobbled path to the door, where another large flagstone formed the step. In the end terrace cottage, next door to the Parkers, lived Mr and Mrs Cooper, a childless couple, then in their fifties. Dick Cooper was the local mole-catcher, a full-time occupation. He went to work on foot most days, with a big bag over his shoulder and his grey Bedlington terrier at his heels. Sometimes, presumably when working on outlying farms, he rode a bicycle which he wheeled from a wooden shed at the end of the path which went along the side of the house; then the dog trotted after him. Mrs Cooper rarely went beyond the garden, and used the back door rather than the front, which was always closed. Every morning she would scuttle with a bucket of soapy water, her pinafore protected by a sacking apron, to scrub the front doorstep and the one by the gate, finishing them with a white edging from a scouring-stone. This daily ritual irritated my mother, who was not committed to scrubbing doorsteps and felt that the woman had too little to do.

Next door to the Coopers lived Mrs Metcalfe, with her daughter Elsie, who was fourteen when my father came to the school. She was a delightful, child-like, friendly girl, who didn't go out to work and enjoyed playing folk tunes and popular melodies on the piano. 'Uncle Arthur', Arthur Robinson, lived with them, a widower whose only son had died as a toddler from sucking phosphorus-tipped matches. He was brother to 'Uncle Jack' Robinson, who lived with his wife, 'Aunt Edie', in a substantial cottage on the other side of the Parkers' house. The honorary relationship was for Elsie's benefit and they were all great friends. Mrs Metcalfe was called Dot by Aunt Edie, a bustling, handsome, dark-haired Londoner with flashing black eyes, who'd kept her cockney accent. She wore crisp, clean pinafores. I believe she met her husband when she came into service at Kirby Hall in Lord Knaresborough's time; Jack still worked for Mr Penty, who bought the old estate. They had a comfortably furnished, well polished home, a very large and beautifully kept garden, and no children. Edie beat a trail to Mrs Metcalfe's several times a day, sometimes carrying covered bowls or plates, and Dot would go in the opposite direction on a similar errand.

Mrs Metcalfe was positively my favourite person in the village. She was under five feet tall, slightly hunch-backed, having been dropped as a baby, so she said, and was the first adult I outgrew. She was a bundle of energy, with broad hands and flat, spade-like finger ends, and a rich and ready laugh. When I was quite small she opened a shop in her front room, conveniently opposite the school gate. A board was attached to the wall: 'E. Metcalfe, licensed to sell sweets and tobacco'. She soon began to make bread to sell: large white loaves, a few brown loaves, and well-fruited currant teacakes. She and Elsie got up at four o'clock in the morning and baked them in the fire-oven attached to her kitchen range. By mid-morning the shop smelt of new bread and she would come in to serve, wiping floury hands on her apron, her face rosy from the heat. I enjoyed the occasions when my mother and I went through into the crowded little kitchen, with Elsie or Uncle Arthur in the alcove under the stairs and Smutty, the completely black cat, on a cushioned stool by the fire. I was warned not to stroke Smutty because she would scratch, but I admired her and longed to cuddle her. Sometimes Aunt Edie would be in the shop, relishing village gossip; sometimes Elsie would be practising on the piano behind the counter and would turn on the piano stool and join the conversation. Neither she nor Aunt Edie served.

Mrs Metcalfe enjoyed selling sweets to children. For a halfpenny you could buy a cone-shaped bag with two ounces of dolly mixtures, jelly babies or wine gums, weighed in the stout metal scale with its polished brass pan and weights. A larger one held a pennyworth, four ounces. She would usually put a few extra in when the scales had gone down. Most of the sweets were in large glass jars, on the window sill, on a shelf in the alcove, or even on top of the piano. They included Bassett's liquorice allsorts, Pontefract cakes, Fox's glacier mints, mixed toffees with coloured foil wrappers, mint humbugs, pear drops and cough drops. Aniseed balls were twenty a penny. The counter was full of delights, such as liquorice bootstraps, tubes of fruit gums and pastilles, chocolate bars, sherbet fountains, packets of lemonade crystals with dippers of boiled sugar on white sticks, and foul-tasting, heart-shaped boxes made of soft, pink, sugary paste, with a trinket inside and a decorated hard sugar top. I didn't like the edible boxes, but bought them regularly for the chance of a new ring, and ate them because they were there. There was chewing gum, too, in strips or sugar-coated pieces, and big wrapped lumps of pink bubble gum, smelling like the tiny squashed flies that you poked from your eyes on summer evenings, and tasting just like it smelled; huge gob-stoppers could be bought wrapped from the counter, smaller ones from a jar.

In season, she sold leather-thonged whips with wooden handles, and tops, cone-shaped and ridged or slender-waisted with a wide head. The two designs needed different techniques of wrapping and whipping. When the marble season began she sold 'stonies' and the beautifully marked glass creations known as 'glass alleys'. Stonies were twenty a penny from a large jar, 'glassies' came in packets of eight, with a cellophane window to tempt you with their colours and patterns. Stonies, made of baked clay, coloured and dipped in glaze, were expendable; they lacked character, were liable to crack, cheap to replace; but I fell in love with my glassies and was reluctant to chance losing them in the school yard, preferring to hoard them to play with after school or on winter evenings on the front room carpet. They are still in their velvet bag and I would hate to part with them because some became old friends; I can even remember the people I won the most prized ones from. The duller browns were worth venturing on the chance of winning a beauty and some blues were a bit ordinary. Mrs Metcalfe always had more, but, like any object I possessed and contemplated with pleasure, I always treasured them, even if they became scarred by the rough school yard. That's why I keep so many worn-out geraniums now; they have the gnarled beauty of old friends.

Mrs Metcalfe sold 'pop', too; cream soda and dandelion and burdock, limeade and lemonade, made by Mustills of Roecliffe, near Boroughbridge. A familiar sound was the tinkling of cases of bottles being unloaded from the delivery wagon, a pickup-sized old blue van with a chugging engine. Shop closing hours must have been bedtime, because my uncles and I often went across on summer evenings, after playing cricket in the field, for a refreshing bottle of creamy-headed dandelion and burdock, and some twopenny packets of Smith's crisps, with their blue paper screws of salt.

The Clarkson family lived next to the shop. Their two children, Fred and Kathleen, were several years younger than me. When the children were in bed, Mr and Mrs Clarkson would stroll down the village, arm in arm, for a short walk. Harry Clarkson was handsome, quiet, relaxed, a former widower fifteen years older than his wife, but she had the hassle of motherhood. As the children grew bigger and naughtier, Mrs Clarkson would chase them round the cottages at bedtime on summer evenings, wielding a stick. I treasure the memory of her saying to my mother on one such evening when we were in the front garden, 'Eh, they're fair fon' brazzen are t'kids,' as she herded them indoors. Although officially settled, they would hang out of the bedroom window, laughing, when their parents had gone for a walk, and dive back smartly when they were in sight again. This appeared to be the extent of their rebellion and no shrieks or screams or raised voices emerged from the family home. As the children grew older they were an affectionate, close-knit family, eventually moving to a council house in Branton. When we came back to live in Dunsforth I sometimes met Mrs Clarkson, by then a widow, and she loved to chat about the time when we were neighbours. Kathleen became a bus conductress, married a builder, and lived in a pleasant new house in Branton near her mother; Fred left the village to work elsewhere.

The cottage at the far end of the row was home to Mrs Charlie Robinson. I don't remember her husband, a retired policeman and no relation to Arthur and Jack, but she was one of the few people I would talk to. I loved going to visit her, always with my mother, but we went more regularly into her home than into most others. She had never learned to read and write, but experience had brought her serenity and wisdom. She had given birth to ten children, 'four boys and then a gal, then four more boys and another gal'. Mary Cocker, her youngest, who lived in Little Ouseburn, was the mother of Ronnie, Peggy and John. Ronnie was my age, in the same class, and they all came regularly with their mother to visit their grandma. On fine days, while Mary was in the house, the children would sit on the front wall, swinging their legs and waiting to be called in for tea. Several of Mrs Robinson's sons had been of military age during the First World War and two had been killed in action. Their fading sepia photographs, taken in uniform, were on the dresser in her living room – handsome young men. I never knew where the surviving sons and older daughter lived, but at least one son visited her by car.

She augmented her pension by making rag rugs. People gave her colourful old clothes and a large sack which had been unpicked and washed and, for £1, she could turn it within a week, or a fortnight at the most, into an artistic rug, in well balanced patches of colour with the conventional black border and a wide band of fabric on the underside to give the edges strength when it was being shaken. She cut the cloth into strips, cut the strips into lengths of about two and a half inches, slightly on the diagonal to facilitate 'pricking', and sorted them into bags of individual colours and mixtures. She used a meat skewer to prick holes in the sacking, pushed the pieces, one at a time, through to the underside with the aid of the skewer, and poked them through again from the back, pulling the two ends even. She also made smaller bedroom rugs by unpicking worn-out knitted garments and pricking bunches of curled knitting yarn through finely woven sacking. These were in pastel colours, usually of mixed content because wool garments shrank and became matted, and totally backed with fabric. They lasted well, in spite of being prone to losing a few threads and some of their curl. The rag rugs were much more durable. My mother and I made smaller ones ourselves; very pleasurable it was, too, and satisfying to have something so attractive and useful made from what could have been thrown away.

When we visited her we always sat in the living room facing the road. She had a rocking chair by the fire and near the window, where she sat, often with the rug she was making spread across her knees. She had no fixed pattern, but started at one end and worked across, making squares, triangles, and areas of in-filling as she went. She marked the centre, where there was always a brightly coloured circle, edged with black, and worked towards it, edging each shape with black and distributing the geometrical shapes with the unerring artistry of long experience. While she was working she kept an eye on passers-by. She missed nothing of interest or note. I well remember one occasion when a young woman was passing, newly married:

'She'll be expectin', ah reckon. She's getten t'creddle cough already. Silly little thing, she's nobbut eighteen,' the 'cradle cough' being that give-away sickly stomach cough of early pregnancy.

On the window sill was a beautifully nurtured hydrangea with a fluted cover pot decorated with flowers. It had been a gift from Mrs Ellison. The Ellisons were jewellers from Leeds, who often came by car on Sundays. It was a family friendship, probably through one of her older sons. Both were small and plump. He had a gold watch chain across his well-rounded waistcoat and she wore lacy jumpers with strings of pearls, and long ear-rings. Her greyish-yellow hair was piled in a bun on top of her head and wispy strands drifted from it into the nape of her neck. The plant grew well and flowered over several seasons:

'Look at mi changeable, its oppenin' well now. They call it "right changeable", yer know, because it cums out green and pink and then goes blue,' a reasonable interpretation of the name by someone who couldn't read.

When Mrs Robinson was well into her seventies and a little less active, my mother used to go across regularly to read the Sunday paper to her. There was always a horoscope by 'Lyndoe', which she took fairly seriously, and she liked to comment on the articles of general interest, and just chat. There was a delightfully relaxed atmosphere in that cottage, and a cosy smell of old polished furniture warmed by the fire.

My parents had known her husband, and I remember her arriving at our back door one morning carrying two Staffordshire dogs. Apparently 'Robi'son' had told her before he died that she must give them to Mr Nicholl on her seventieth birthday, because he liked these ornaments. My dad had previously bought from them the piece entitled *Mary II*, which I now keep in my study. They must have had a very good feeling towards him to part with it, and I shall always have a special regard for that and the dogs, as well as a small ornamental cup and saucer that she gave me quite spontaneously one day just as we were leaving. It stood on the dresser, along with other pieces of pottery and the photographs of her soldier sons. A photograph taken to celebrate her eightieth birthday shows the person I remember so well, a serene countrywoman who had experienced adversity and joy and accepted all with natural dignity and grace.

The second group of Pope's cottages, beyond the yard and Miss Peach's house, were down a short, unmade lane. Mr and Mrs Ibbotson and their only daughter, Doreen, two years older than me, lived in the first one, and the third was occupied by an elderly widower we rarely saw. But it was the second one that we visited. Mr and Mrs Smith (Ruth and Arthur) lived there; she was the school caretaker and Mr Smith helped her by doing the outside work of sweeping the yards, stoking the boiler and cleaning the toilet blocks. She was still in her late thirties, fluffy-haired and pretty, with a rich and ready laugh; he was in his fifties, a small, thin man and former jockey. He worked part-time for the Jacksons as a farm labourer. The only son still living with them was Jimmy, the youngest, who was in my dad's class. Agnes, a thin and rather elegant girl, left school at around the time my parents moved to Ouseburn and started training as a nurse in Harrogate when she was seventeen. She married Harry Knowles before she qualified, and was the mother of Sylvia and Michael. She died quite young, shortly after we went to live in Dunsforth. The Smiths' older son, Jack, was in the army; the older daughter, Daisy, small, well rounded and friendly, married a sergeant-major, Tom Smith, a large, dark-haired, red-faced man with a prominent military chest. She spent a lot of time with her parents when her husband was serving abroad and was there during her first pregnancy. After Gwennie was born we were invited in to see the baby. I was intrigued by the breast-feeding and back-rubbing, but uneasy when the small, floppy scrap was put into my arms. So was Gwennie!

My mother and I were always welcome in their cottage and of course one or both were around the school every day. Mrs Smith, particularly, was someone I warmed to and another of the few people who could get a word out of me. She was happy for me to stand and watch when she was cleaning the classrooms or scrubbing the cloakroom floors. I don't think I said very much, but she kept up a companionable flow of chatter. My conversations with Mr Smith were more limited:

'Nah, Maargrit.'

'Now then, Mr Smith.'

Are yer all reet, then?'

'Yes, thank you.'

On one memorable occasion he was raking the gravel path in the garden for my Dad and I'd been picking flowers and was standing watching him. An earwig fell out onto the ground:

'Yer'd better be careful yer don't get one o' them in yer ear. Yer wouldn't 'alf know about it.' My stomach jerked with revulsion and I've hated them ever since.

These, then, were our immediate neighbours, but the village shops and shopkeepers were very much part of our everyday lives. Mr and Mrs Waddington (Tommy and Ethel) owned a seventeenth-century cottage and a few acres of land on the right hand side as you went up the village from the school house. They sold milk and cream and had a shop, later Mrs Porter's, in the front room. We got our milk from them, delivered warm from the cow milked by Tommy Waddington's calloused, farmerly hands. It came in lidded aluminium cans, cylindrical with narrower necks, quart size, pint size or gill size. Jimmy Smith came jangling down the village every morning and evening after milking time, with two handfuls of milk cans. If we wanted cream, we took our jug to the shop and Mrs Waddington went out to the dairy and skimmed some off.

The Waddingtons' shop couldn't have been more different in atmosphere from Mrs Metcalfe's. It was a spacious room, with a door through which you could glimpse the dark, sunless living quarters. The brass bell rang when you entered. Occasionally, Mr Waddington would serve, in his working clothes, but usually Mrs Waddington came. You had to wait until she abandoned what she was doing and shuffled slowly into the shop, shoes flapping on the worn square red tiles. She was an ageless woman, probably in her late fifties or even sixty, pear-shaped, lethargic and bleak, with a creaking voice and humourless manner, in spite of going through the motions of smiling and being helpful. Her slightly furry face and the coarse hairs on her chin and upper lip, exaggerated in my childish perception, gave me the impression of rind, like the cheese covered in muslin that stood on the counter. I hated waiting there while she made conversation with my mother. I hated it even more when I was old enough to be sent on errands and had to communicate directly.

Although the shop was on the sunny side of the street, it always seemed chilly and smelt of a mixture of old walls and new foodstuffs, particularly bacon, resting on the slicer near the scales. She sold some sweets, but mostly general groceries and tinned goods. Sugar, flour, currants and raisins were weighed out from bulk containers and packed in blue or brown paper bags. She was very careful to let the scale barely fall, and the quickest movement she made was in whipping off the weighed goods as soon as the pan moved downwards. I remember one occasion when she actually broke a large muscatel raisin in half because the scale went down too quickly with the whole raisin in. It seemed appropriate that she sold scouring blocks, carbolic soap, dried peas with steeping tablets, and unpleasant things like packets of highly spiced Symingtons' soup powder. The peas were all right: the packets contained nets to boil them in; these could be stitched to a rounded piece of thick wire, pushed into the end of a garden cane, and used for tiddler fishing. Our most valued acquisition from the Waddingtons was a tortoiseshell cat, Impy, who presented us with two kittens, Horme and Mneme, in a box in the wash kitchen, and started the family dynasty of weirdly-named and eccentric felines, but that was much later.

A little further up the street was Burrell's yard, with the policeman's house on one corner and Watsons' shop on the other. The smell and atmosphere of Watsons' shop was different again and also distinctive. It was floored with thick boards, protected near the door by a large mat, and had a high counter of polished wood. A cupboard of toiletries and patent medicines, essentially a chemist's shop, stood on the opposite wall, and a cabinet of reels of cotton and other sewing accessories occupied the left hand corner of the counter, facing the door. Draperies, from tea-towels and dusters to socks and aprons, hung from lengths of clothes line strung across the same area, keeping out some light from the front window and darkening the counter. Tinned goods lined the shelves behind the counter and bulk goods stood on the floor ready for weighing. The business side of the counter held the scales, the bacon slicer and a large cheese board with a wire and marble slab. Butter and other perishable goods were kept cool in a pantry near the door from the house; whoever served popped out to fetch them. On the right hand side of the shop, attractive in the light from a smaller window, was a table full of sweets. The counter had a lift-up section to enable Mr or Mrs Watson to serve these and the toiletries and patent medicines.

The Watsons, another childless couple in their fifties, had their own business style. Mrs Watson was small, dark, round and pinafored, with the bustling air of one who has been called from more important activities to which she couldn't wait to return; but nevertheless, she could gossip. I didn't take much notice of the grown-ups' talk, but I have the impression that she grumbled; I would stand shifting from one leg to the other, contemplating the goods in the shop, the floor boards, her hair slides and the streaks of grey in her hair, her round face and glasses above a short neck, and waiting for the conversation to end. 'Sad' Watson, in his brown overall, served the customers with a slow, leisurely timelessness that hung in the air, but he chatted less than his wife and we were served and departed after the formal exchange of pleasantries. 'Sad' was not a reflection of his personality, though it suited his pleasant, long, solemn face – neither he nor his wife radiated humour; it was because he was also the village saddler. In retrospect, the characteristic smell of the shop owed something to leather and pipe tobacco. When I was sent on an errand I would peer over the counter at Mr Watson's serious face and make my request, such as, 'Please may Mommy have half a pound of New Zealand butter and a tube of Euthymol toothpaste?' I had always been told precisely what to say, so that I should be seen as a polite little girl. After passing him the coins, embarrassingly hot from my careful clutches, I would scuttle out again. I dawdled to the shop and ran all the way home.

The policeman's house on the opposite corner had a black notice board, headed 'West Riding Constabulary', in its narrow front garden. Often it was bare, but occasionally notices in fine print appeared and lingered there, curling and fading. On one occasion it held a big red warning of restrictions because of foot and mouth disease. I was older then and on my way to the school bus. As a young child going on errands I passed it with a tremor of acknowledgement that it represented authority. 'Bobby' Teale, a cheerful man with a purplish nose and cheeks threaded with broken capillaries, was occasionally to be seen in uniform riding his bike through the village. He must have had an easy life in this law-abiding community, even though he was responsible for several villages. I imagine bureaucracy was his worst headache.

Burrell's yard was a male domain, though there were two cottages next to the Watsons' shop and a right of way through it to a back lane and the Oddfellows' allotments. Billy Burrell was the village joiner and undertaker and a skilled craftsman. He ran his business from a large, open-fronted shed, full of planks, saw-horses, shavings, sawdust, and workmen shouting good-humouredly to each other over the whining of the big circular saw. It was one of my father's favourite yarning places: 'I'm just going up to Billy Burrell's for half a pint of nails,' – or, 'some putty and glass to mend the cold frame'. He used a lot of nails for minor repairs, particularly to old seed boxes once the bedding plants had outgrown the greenhouse. Nothing would be thrown away if it could be patched up. The workshop was one of the few places where he could indulge his love of 'men's talk', jokes and backchat; it always took a long time to measure out nails.

The Burrells lived in a house at the side of the path, near the shed. Occasionally, my mother and I would have a few words with Mrs Burrell in passing by on our way to the back lane, and sometimes we'd be invited in for a cup of tea and cake or biscuits. She was a waddling, slightly breathless, barrel-shaped, well-corseted woman with several chins, a high colour, and sparse, greying hair pulled back in a bun. She wore the conventional everyday clothing of many country women, a black skirt with grey stripes, knitted jumper, and apron stretched tightly across her vast stomach. She radiated kindliness, welcome and good humour. They had one son, George, who followed his father into the business and was undertaker for my father's funeral.

From an early age George hung around with the workmen and became, shall we say, knowledgeable beyond his years. There's a lovely story, probably told with pride to my dad, of one occasion when the vicar called. Mr Burrell was a churchwarden and pillar of the community; the incumbent was very much a 'dear vicar', with the voice, accent and manner of a social superior among the peasantry. Picture a cameo of village hospitality along these lines:

'Do come in and have some tea, Vicar, and a bite to eat.'

'Oh, thank you so much, Mrs Burrell; I'd love to.'

Polite conversation follows and a cup of tea is dispensed in the best china.

'Now, what will you have to eat? A scone and jam? Chocolate cake? Or shall I make you a ham sandwich?'

'Oh, er, well, really I don't know what to say. You are so kind!'

Voice from the corner as four-year-old George looks up from his toys:

'Boil 't'bugger an egg.'

The familiar village where I felt most at home extended only to the top of the hill. What lay beyond the church and Church Lane was out of sight of the bedroom window that overlooked the village street. It was another country, to be entered reluctantly, particularly if we were going to the post office. Mrs Jackson ran the post office in the old manor house where later the Meeks had their garage. It seems strange, in retrospect that she was another person who frightened me, but the features which gave the building its historic interest were intimidating and she was inseparable from them. The heavy, studded door with its cold metal sneck, the bell echoing through the darkness of the entrance, the almost empty space, the large, square, red tiles, worn by years of treading, the high counter with its mesh guard at one side, the chill that came from its position on the sunless side of the street, all created an unwelcoming atmosphere. We waited by the counter until she came through from the house, stood behind it and said, 'Yes?' in a deep voice that resonated through the shop. She would exchange pleasantries with my mother, but to me, standing by impatiently, it seemed that there was nothing to linger for, nothing interesting to buy. She sold extras such as writing paper and envelopes, but there were no shelves packed with goods, and rarely did another customer come in while we were there. To someone small, lingering in the chill shadows, it was a joyless place from which to escape to the freedom and brightness of the street.

The post office was her only business. Her brother, Jack Bell, was the postman. He was a welcome sight, as he propped his official red bike against walls while he delivered letters and parcels. He would wobble down the footpath a few yards at a time between the houses, he would balance the weight of the heavy mail bag in the basket in front, and return to the office at a good pace when it was empty. I never knew Mrs Jackson's background. I think she and her brother lived together; her son, reputed to be 'wild', had already left home, was living in London, and visited occasionally; her husband had long gone into the twilight world of muted adult conversation.

Her sister, Mrs Richardson, as friendly as Mrs Jackson seemed remote, lived in Starra Cottage, then the last house on the left below the school. The Richardsons kept poultry in part of the large garden, and sold eggs. I enjoyed visiting Mrs Richardson to buy eggs, because we were sometimes taken into the poultry run behind the house to collect the eggs, and invited into the house for tea and cake. In the garden, near the path to the gate, was a roofed, brick well, covered in ivy-leaved toadflax, with a handle to turn the wooden roller that controlled the rope attached to the bucket. Sometimes I was allowed to turn the handle, with help, and raise a bucketful to pour into another container to fill the water trough in the hen pen. Wilf Richardson, a kind, quiet man, kept the vegetable garden immaculate and grew enormous sweet peas; he was Miss Thompson's gardener, and was usually working when we called.

Mrs Richardson died when I was in my teens, but I came to appreciate Mrs Jackson when we lived in Upper Dunsforth. She had retired to the cottage next door to her brother-in-law's father, old Mr Richardson, and was a familiar figure striding out towards Ouseburn to what was, by that time, the combined general store and post office run by the Hindmarsh family. She was chatty and friendly and gave Chrissie the spotted crake which her son had bought in the auction of Lord Knaresborough's estate in 1919. Whenever I hear the first blackbird singing, I remember the joy on her face one mild morning in February. She remarked that the blackbird was singing early and said how much she always looked forward to hearing its song as a sign of spring. As my childhood bogeywoman, though, she rivalled Miss Peach.

In the 1930s, the shop eventually owned by the Hindmarshes was run by Ethel and Charlie Dodgson. It was the largest in the village, well stocked with a variety of hardware, such as wicker baskets, as well as the essential groceries and homely remedies for minor ailments and digestive problems. It was convenient for people living at the Branton end of the village, but we usually shopped nearer home. Ethel, a single woman in her twenties, niece to Mrs Waddington, had the pear-shaped family figure, and characteristic dry voice; her brother, Charlie, who later serviced and sold cars, spent his time between the shop and his father's business across the road. The Dodgsons were quite affluent in village terms. Their detached family house had an annexe where Ben Dodgson, a skilled cobbler, repaired shoes and stout work boots with their rows of hobnails and steel toe and heel plates. The shelves at the back were filled with boxes of men's, women's and children's shoes and slippers, and there were rows of wellingtons on the floor. The working area contained a heavy-duty sewing machine and a cluttered bench under the window arrayed with lasts, hammers, knives and other tools. The long counter, behind which he perched on a stool to work, contained footwear awaiting repair or collection, with a space in the middle for serving customers. When we went in, he would look up over his glasses and heavy, grizzled moustache from the boot between his leather-aproned legs, where he would be hammering in nails or paring the sole to size. He would smile a cheerful greeting and stop work to serve us. On one occasion my mother bought me a pair of shiny patent leather, ankle-strap shoes and I skipped all the way home, proudly wearing them. I always enjoyed taking shoes to be mended or collecting repairs.

Now a short digression before I complete the picture of village businesses. When my parents first came to Great Ouseburn there was no public transport. People thought nothing of walking to Boroughbridge, or even the eight miles to Knaresborough market along a short cut up Moor Lane to the Great North Road and through Arkendale and Ferrensby, and returning at the end of the day carrying their purchases. For a small fee one could ride, legs dangling over the side, alongside the parcels on Jim Jennison's carrier's cart to join the York-Harrogate train at Cattal station, returning the same way, or one could walk the three miles. Around 1930, however, the United Bus Company began to run a service through the villages between Ripon and York, via Boroughbridge. The bus stop was at 'Swann's corner', the junction between Carr Side and the main street, where the blacksmith's forge stood. Its shoeing shed and workshop overlooked the village green on one side; round the corner, where the bus stopped, were his house and a little shop where he and his wife sold ironmongery and other necessities for farmers and handymen, another of my dad's yarning-places when Harold was serving. Shortly afterwards, the West Yorkshire Road Car Company started a daily service to Knaresborough and Harrogate, which terminated at the village green. By 1936 this gave access to the Knaresborough and Harrogate Grammar schools and the Roman Catholic school in Harrogate.

My warm feelings towards Harold Swann and the blacksmith's workshop belong, then, to a period beyond my early education at the village school when, for eight years, I travelled on the bus to Knaresborough and waited for it by the forge. It was a snout-nosed twenty-five-seater, nicknamed 'the little pig', operated by a driver who also took fares. We schoolchildren got to know the friendly team of drivers very well, particularly Jack, who would tease us and swoop over the two 'bumps' – humpy hills on the way to Coneythorpe. Although it was a public service bus, few village people used it, except on Wednesdays, when two farmers' wives, Mrs Harrison and Mrs Elgie, mother and daughter, regularly took their covered baskets of produce to sell on the long stall set aside for local farmers' wives at Knaresborough market, where they all stood side by side, selling butter and home-made cakes, jams and pickles, even eggs. The two women always occupied double seats at the front and conversed across the aisle, or rather, Mrs Harrison talked, punctuating her sentences with, 'In't it, Annie?', or 'Di'n't we, Annie?', and Annie replied, 'Aye.'

The few pupils from the Ouseburns who used the school bus gathered in the wide, concreted area leading to the open-fronted shoeing shed shortly before ten past eight, standing alongside the farm implements waiting for repair, or sheltering in the shed. Early morning was a favoured time for shoeing, before work in the fields began, so that quite often a cart-horse would be tethered already in the shed, and the door to the adjoining forge with its furnace and anvil would be open, the familiar stench of burning horse hoof mingling with the sharp, steamy, manure-rich smell of a working horse; the busy ringing of hammer on metal would echo around the village green.

Whenever it was cold or wet we were allowed to shelter in the shed alongside the blinkered horse where, through the doorway to the forge itself, we could watch Harold working and enjoy the warmth from the fire. The workshop was dark and cavernous, hung about with equipment to be mended or collected, full of mysterious shapes, illuminated mainly by the fire. I don't know how far shoes were reused; there were plenty hanging around the walls, but sometimes he would blow the embers to white heat, thrust in a bar of iron, withdraw it, white hot onto the anvil, hammer it into a bevelled shape, clip off sufficient for a shoe and bend it over the point of the anvil. It was like a painting in motion: the glowing fire waiting to be called sharply to life by the bellows, waist high, no impression of its surroundings, just a hollow, glowing red, outlining the anvil; then with a blast from the bellows, the brilliant light, the white-hot metal, Harold's strong features, shining with sweat, plucking the shoe from the fire, hammering it, sparks flying, to its final shape and size, punching holes, dunking it, sizzling, into a tub of water.

We would stand back as he carried it with tongs into the shoeing shed, lifted the horse's foot, held it firmly between his knees and pressed the new shoe to the hoof, bitter smoke rising, to singe the pattern of its final position onto the hoof; then more checking, paring, filing and, if necessary another visit to the anvil, before he finally hammered in the nails, curled them over the side of the hoof with the claw of the hammer, released the foot. After a few encouraging words to the horse, which would sometimes be restive and unwilling to raise a leg, he would tug its shaggy fetlock, set the next foot between his knees, inspect the hoof, hook off the old shoe with pliers, its nails still hanging, and pare away the surplus growth ready to repeat the process. There was no conversation; we just stood watching him work, speedily and deftly, to make sure the horse was ready for its day in the fields. We rarely saw the farmer collect his horse; we were speeding along the road to Marton-cum-Grafton.

When Harold retired, some years later, shire horses were no longer the mainstay of farming and the business was relying more on repairing machinery. Elliot, the younger son, developed it into one of the foremost agricultural engineering firms in the neighbourhood, selling as well as maintaining machinery, and he and his family were still there when we left Dunsforth. It remains 'Swann's Corner'.

CHAPTER IV

The village school

While I was still at home with my mother the school was an overbearing stone presence shading the kitchen, a creature of moods, to be tiptoed round during the day, approached with uncertainty when temporarily it became an empty shell. We lived on the fringes, round the side, behind our gate. The school bell summoned the dawdlers twice a day. They scuttled down the street, rushed into the yard, and were consumed. Then the whole body began to rumble: prayers and hymns, times-tables and spellings, poetry and sing-song repetition, music and singing, authoritative voices, subsiding to an instructive monologue, my father's, 'You silly, idle monkeys!' rising to a shout towards the end of the afternoon. Sporadically, and for varying lengths of time, it spewed out the older boys into the yard, where they hurtled round in the corner by our kitchen window, screeched, shouted, tumbled in piles in the dust, slid on sparking hobnails, before meekly forming lines and being absorbed again. They were physically intrusive, unlike the girls and small boys in the other playground. At half-past three, briefly the clatter of chairs being inverted on the desks, the murmuring of a prayer – then a quick evacuation, the clang of a bucket and scrape of furniture, and finally silence. My father, too, disappeared at ten minutes to nine, reappeared at playtimes and dinner time and emerged at the end of the day to bring in the drinking water, trim the paraffin lamps, clean the wicks and refill the bottle of paraffin at the end of the cooking stove, replenish the coal buckets, bring in wood. These tasks complete he would sit by the fire so that I could climb onto his knee to be entertained until teatime.

The infants' classroom was a comparatively recent addition to the nineteenth-century building with its high-ceilinged double room divided by a screen, and arched windows. The girls' cloakroom had doors to all three classrooms currently in use. On the other side, the boys' cloakroom gave access to the main double room and a spare classroom. During the Second World War the latter became the school canteen, but at this time it was known as the 'cod liver oil room', because it housed the cupboard with big bottles of cod liver oil, a box of distinctive oval ginger biscuits, and an enamelled jug of non-stainless, fishy teaspoons from which to feed the sickly golden liquid at afternoon playtime into the open mouths of those whose parents could afford to pay the necessary twopence-halfpenny a week, quite a commitment for larger families. The room also contained the weight-scale, with its iron stand, fine-tuned balance and sliding weights, because the school doctor based herself there for her annual visit, and the village nurse inspected heads there and examined any child giving cause for concern. It gave my father privacy to talk to visitors such as Mr Ludford, the attendance officer, known as the 'kid-catcher', who came on his motor bike in leather coat, plus fours and a cap with ear muffs, or the divisional clerk, Mr Hall, in grey suit, grey, fitted overcoat and trilby hat, who came by car. On these occasions his class celebrated his absence in the usual way and attracted the wrath of the teacher in the junior room.

I don't know how often I went into the building in these early years; it settled into my bones gradually when, as an older child, I explored its emptiness and made it mine. This joy of possession grew in the longer days, always summer, always bright. I homed in on the infants' classroom with its glowing warmth and lingering smells of plasticine, children's bodies, and chalk dust, the motes dancing in shafts of late-afternoon sunlight. The attraction there was the library box, which catered for the whole age range. It was part of the West Riding's education service to schools, delivered once a term; lifting the lid of a new library box, with its distinctive smell of wood and used books, was as good as Christmas. Officially, Miss Dawson kept the record of borrowings, but I didn't bother to take anything out; I spent the hour between school and teatime curled up on the floor there, reading stories by Angela Brazil about the misdeeds of the upper fourth in some enviable boarding school and their crushes on attractive prefects. There I first met *Little Women*, *Anne of Green Gables*, Brer Fox and Brer Rabbit, *Uncle Tom's Cabin* and *Black Beauty*. I read anything and everything except the adventures of Doctor Dolittle, which were supposed to be funny, but I found utterly stupid; the man was a fool. The box provided me with a supplement to the fairy tales, myths and legends, poetry, classical novels and *Children's Encyclopaedia* we had in the house, and was the foundation for my lifelong comfort habit of reading fiction for relaxation.

The friendliness of my father's room drew me; I felt free to sit at the desk, read the mirror writing on the blotter, dip the pen into the inkwell, admire his ornate signature on the correspondence awaiting posting, and his flourishing style of addressing envelopes with the stamp awry in the top corner. I measured my height on the ruled strip fixed on the side of the cupboard and explored the cupboard itself for books and new pencils. There, in due course I found classics for the older children's reading: *Ivanhoe* and novels by Sir Walter Scott to supplement those we had in the house, Fenimore Cooper's *Last of the Mohicans* and Robert Louis Stevenson's *Treasure Island* and *Kidnapped*.

When Mrs Smith came to sweep the floors I would hear the clattering of her metal dustpan and brushes on the floor of the boys' cloakroom. If quietly reading a library book, I would stay for a while, knowing she wouldn't come in until she'd cleaned the other rooms. My father's room was nearer and, if I didn't feel inclined to talk, I would creep out by the door leading to the girls' yard.

At the bottom of the girls' yard, metal railings and a railed gate closed off the steps to the boiler room, or 'stoke 'ole' where, for much of the school year, the huge, black, cast-iron boiler, its heat shimmering in the dust-laden air, gave off choking sulphurous fumes. Wide pipes of circulating water, bent into angles, led up through the ceiling into the classrooms, circling the walls and providing hot seats on wet winter playtimes. As I grew older, I was able to open the creaking gate and was no longer afraid of descending the steep, mossy steps and opening the door to the alien region below. Distorted clinkers were heaped on the floor beside the hole from which they had been raked; the furnace, radiating heat, was safely contained behind its iron door; the stock of coke stood in a pile where it had been shovelled down two chutes from the corner of the yard. The boiler fascinated me, and after school I often crept down there into its warm and gloomy cave, ignoring the sulphurous dust and rank, bitter smell of the coke pile, with a tremulous feeling that perhaps I shouldn't be there alone, though nobody had forbidden me to go. I felt more at ease when Mr Smith was raking out the clinker and ash and stoking the boiler; then its mouth was open, with bright fire glowing within or blue flames licking over red embers. The cold coke deadened the fire, the door was shut, the ash and clinker tidied away. One year, shortly before Christmas, I noticed Mrs Smith sitting near the boiler plucking geese for some farmer's orders. I went down and stood watching and talking to her as she worked, plucking out stubborn feathers and tidying up the remaining quills, until the only feathers left were those on the neck, which dangled between her knees above the purple head and sightless eyes, while the pile of feathers grew beside her and tiny wisps of down floated in the warm currents of air, fringing her hair, clinging to her cheeks and tickling my nostrils. In summer, the boiler stood cold, clean and empty, the depleted coke pile neatly swept back, until the new load of coke arrived in September and the monster came to life again.

In 1932 my father got permission to put up his own greenhouse in the corner of the garden near the girls' yard. Its boiler, which circulated hot water, was heated conveniently by a coke fire, and it was a comfortable work place and refuge. Shortly afterwards he persuaded the West Riding to buy a rectangular piece of land to extend the school property from the top end of the girls' yard and small garden, in order to teach gardening to the senior boys and girls. The authority provided basic equipment and the plot was turned into a large vegetable garden with cold frames, soft fruit and cordon apple trees. Half-hardy annual bedding plants, raised in the greenhouse and hardened off in the cold frames, were sold by the score in the village to offset expenses, and he could easily sell all he grew.

The greenhouse was my dad's personal domain, where he spent many comfortable hours. He welcomed my presence there and taught me how to dust chrysanthemums with flowers of sulphur from a rabbit's tail, remove side-shoots from tomato plants and tap their sticks in the middle of the day to shake the pollen, prick out seedlings into rows with a pencil in shallow fruit boxes, with troughs formed by laying the pencil between the rows to avoid getting water onto the tender plants and causing them to damp off. My mother's help was welcome too, particularly at this busy time of year; but primarily it was where he could sit, comfortably alone, to smoke, meditate and plan. Whenever we went round, to take him a cup of tea or tell him the meal was ready, he would be just sitting, enjoying the orderliness of things growing, pausing to contemplate his next job and admire what had been done. He would say, 'I've just this minute sat me down!' and we would all smile.

In 1937 Donald Cross, whose father had recently come to Branton Green to start a poultry farm, persuaded my dad that it would be a good idea to keep poultry, and an area was wired off across the top of the garden near the field, and along the side next to Wallace Parker's garden where he, also, kept a few hens. Billy Burrell made one hut, and a smaller one covered with roofing felt, with a separate roofed run for shelter in bad weather, was made by one of the older boys, John Hall, who lived up Burrell's yard and intended to become a joiner. We started with a dozen Rhode Island Red hens and a handsome, evil-minded cockerel with long spurs and an insatiable desire to use them to attack small bare knees or the hand that fed him. When driven away with cap or Wellington boot he would retreat to the far corner, shake his feathers and crow defiantly.

Poultry-keeping was entirely unsubsidized by the local authority and didn't make a profit, but it enriched our lives and provided fresh food. The flock was soon extended by allowing broody hens to sit in small coops and raise their own chicks. We acquired two more huts and raised day-old chicks, bought from Thornbers in my father's native Mytholmroyd. I went with him in the sturdy Jowett car to collect them from Cattal station and carried them home on my knee, contentedly listening to their quiet whistling as they huddled in the ventilated box. They spent their first few weeks in the hut on sawdust in a 'hoover', a small zinc-lidded enclosure warmed by a central, specially designed paraffin lamp. The hut was warm, smelling of paraffin, fresh straw and chaff, it was fascinating just to go in there and watch the chicks as they gradually grew feathers and were released from the hoover during the day to scratch about safely in the hut. In the early days they were fed with fine chicken corn, given fresh water, and checked regularly in case one was 'peepy', sitting back on its haunches, distressed and chirping loudly, in need of a warm flannel nest in a basket on top of the boiler by the kitchen fire. Most of these weaklings died, but one raised this way became a long-lived, noisy, wry-necked hen called, predictably, Peepy, who was a good layer in spite of, or perhaps because of, the fact that she couldn't peck straight and was allowed to feed from the measure. We could always recognize her large, slightly ridged egg in the nest-box.

Children who were interested, in practice a few older boys, were encouraged to look after the poultry during their gardening lessons and share the chore of replenishing the water and cleaning out the huts. More huts were added and the original dozen hens became over fifty. Unwanted 'clockers', broody hens with a distinctive 'cluck', were put in battery cages in the back yard for a few days to cool their bodies and so break their desire to brood and bring them back into lay more quickly. We ate surplus cockerels and some old boiling fowls, but the others were collected by a friendly dealer from Leeds, Mr Brash, who came round regularly to local farms and was well respected for his willingness to pay a fair price. Trays of surplus eggs were sold to an agent who collected them from farms on behalf of wholesalers supplying shops in local towns.

The teaching in the senior school now included the various skills needed to maintain a productive garden. When

Boroughbridge Modern School was opened in 1938 my father was asked to advise on the establishment and teaching of rural studies and to mount an exhibition of children's work at the opening ceremony.

The greenhouse, poultry and school garden transformed my childhood, because I learned the skills needed for greenhouse work and poultry-keeping. Over the years I spent a lot of time helping my father, and where I couldn't help I watched and learned. A modest and self-deprecating man, he nevertheless knew exactly what he was doing in the garden. By studying at home, he had taken all the examinations of the Royal Horticultural Society and qualified for their Fellowship. Though I have never used some of the skills he taught me, they are there as part of memory's store, taken out and practised with pleasure in imagination; for example I know exactly how to take and root cuttings of Japanese chrysanthemums, pot them on, disbud them and grow them to produce three or four flowers of exhibition size to enjoy over Christmas and the New Year in the greenhouse, or as cut flowers.

The changes my father made to the school and my love of being alone in the schoolrooms and playgrounds when everyone had gone were in the future on that day in March, 1931 when, to my dismay, the ill-formed, hazy request that was to change my life was acted upon with surprising swiftness. I found myself being escorted across the boys' yard, down the girls' yard, through the cloakroom, into the infants' classroom, to face the stares of around thirty children.

The infants' classroom was where the five to seven years olds were taught in three year groups: second class, first class and standard one. I was seated at a spare desk in second class next to Margery Swann and given a stout cardboard box with metal clips holding its corners, a tight-fitting lid and a memorable board-like smell. It contained coloured, shiny round disks and pieces of card numbered from one to ten. Books I could deal with, but not these objects. Margery was arranging paired disks in columns and putting numbers on the bottom. I looked at this mysterious activity and decided that I would never be able to do that. I picked out disks of the same colour and arranged them in squares and rectangles and ignored the numbers. It was several days before Miss Dawson persuaded me to do anything else with them. I could count, of course, but I cannot recollect the process by which I came to understand the concept of numbers of objects and a symbol to represent this abstract idea, and why these round, shiny playthings were called 'counters'. Reading was familiar and easy and I was already used to forming letters and writing my name, so writing was a pleasure, but not this problematic task.

The classroom was a cheerful place in which to spend the day. The sunny window-sills held cacti, which bloomed gloriously in their season. Children's drawings brightened the walls; the piano stood to the right of the teacher's desk and near the door for ease of wheeling into the next room. A cupboard against the wall adjoining standard one's desks held slates and wooden-backed, thick felt slate-cleaners, coloured chalks, squares of gummed paper in shiny, bright primary colours, plasticine, modelling tools and reading books. It also held our writing books, sum books and the unwelcome boxes of counters. On the front wall, from our point of view in second class, were alphabet pictures, with capital and small letters, drawn and coloured by Miss Dawson so that their shapes resembled the letter they stood for. We used to recite them phonically, making the sound of the letter as it would be said in a word: 'a for apple, b for bat and ball, c for collar, d for duck, e for egg, f for feather, g for glasses', and so on. On the wall behind first class was the calendar and weather chart, a large sheet of drawing paper divided into pencilled squares with the date in one corner. Every day, someone would be chosen to draw the day's weather and write the appropriate description in a space below the picture: sunny, cloudy, windy, raining, snowy. The sky was always at the top of the square and the ground at the bottom, with a gap between for the rest of the picture. I accepted that this was how you drew the outside world, but it was some years before I understood the concept of a horizon.

Second class and standard one sat at paired desks with tip-up bench seats; first class sat centrally in rows on long benches with attached tip-up seats, each place delineated by an incised square of smaller squares, a hole for an inkwell and a groove to hold pencils; we didn't use ink until we were in the juniors. Everyone faced the teaching area at the front, where there was a movable blackboard on its easel.

The classroom was never silent, but there was no audible conversation between neighbours. After our morning Bible story every group was set an activity and Miss Dawson taught each class in turn. For the youngest there might be repetition of the alphabet and counting aloud, writing one's name and reading simple words in big letters from a picture book; for first class, reading stories, learning to write in half exercise books with double green lines for the small letters and red lines above and below for the ones with heads and tails, and simple addition and subtraction; for standard one, reading, writing a diary, and compositions based on earlier teaching. Group instruction involved 'how-to-do-it' addition and subtraction, with carrying or borrowing and paying back, and ultimately, multiplication and division by two or three, the repetition of the necessary times tables and the challenge of adding 'pounds, shillings and pence' using twelves and twenties instead of tens. In the background was the drone of children reading aloud, sounding the letters, struggling with the words. When a problem arose you put up your hand and were called to the teacher's desk; most pupils were called out to the front at some point during the morning session to read or have work marked. Miss Dawson had little patience with silly mistakes and would slap people's hands or legs if she felt they weren't trying hard enough; she was even harsher on those who didn't get on with what they should be doing: she would shout and put a ruler across their hands or legs. It was a tough life for the slow and there was no place at all for fooling or wasting time. I always went apprehensively to the front with racing heart, fearing the worst. She never slapped me, but I was bright compared with many village children, and I was the headmaster's daughter.

Morning playtime provided a diversion in the middle of these activities. At the end of the morning session, we stood, 'hands together, eyes closed', and sang a four-line grace, 'Be present at our table, Lord,' and, before afternoon school, 'We thank thee, Lord, for this our food.' These I could understand once I put aside the thought that my mother was always called 'Bee', but my memory still retains the chancy, off-key version of the tune which sounded loudly from the infants' classroom throughout the whole school just before twelve o'clock and just after one.

Afternoons were the time for geography and history stories, nature study, singing, and communal activities, punctuated by another playtime. We chalked pictures on our small blackboards, cut plasticine with modelling tools and rolled it into animals, cut out patterns from gummed paper and stuck them onto thin card. The older pupils drew with coloured pencils on paper, made simple models and spent more time in silent reading; the big cupboard contained graded reading books, including a series of long, narrow red-backed books with simplified versions of Grimms' fairy tales. The day usually ended with a story read by Miss Dawson. Finally, came the order to stand and tip up the seats of our desks; then a spoken prayer followed. The words of this took a little longer to emerge from confusion than those of the two graces. As far as print can convey, my earliest version, informed by some rudimentary biblical knowledge and a strong feeling for rhythm and emphasis, went something like this:

'O Emily *far-the-wee* thank thee for thy mer *siz* durin' *this* day. We seech thee to keep us in *safe-ty* durin' the *cumminite*. Bless and come for the sick and sore full, and draw Saul nearer to thee, through Jesus Christ our Lord, *our men*.'

Hymns, too, could be puzzling. I couldn't understand why 'Jesus shall rain where'er the sun /Doth his successive journeys run.' From what I'd heard of him it was surprising that he should be such a spoilsport. Neither could I understand why we must pray to be fitted for Heaven 'to live with Theethere'. When I asked my mother who Theethere was, I didn't get a satisfactory answer.

Looking back, I'm not sure whether I really enjoyed my time in the infants' classroom or only felt that I must say I did when asked by adults if I liked school. I accepted it as the way things were, learned quickly, and eventually managed to understand

75

arithmetic, or rather to follow mechanical instructions and get the right answer most of the time. A few things stand out, such as having to remember we had celebrated a New Year and now the day's date at the head of written work was to carry the final number 32 instead of 31. I felt sad at the passing of the old year and a strange apprehension about greeting the new, and a certain pride in carefully writing the date.

As a natural left-hander under relentless pressure from home towards conformity, my failure, in standard one, to make a competent basket out of a sheet of gummed paper was humiliating. Miss Dawson demonstrated each step from the front of the class and we must follow each movement, matching her demonstration to our sheet of paper on the desk in front of us. We had to rule a straight line at one side and cut off a narrow strip for the handle, then fold the paper into sixteen squares and cut up the fold of the two small side squares at each end, fold them over, wet the gum with our tongues to make them stick, thus forming the ends of the basket, and then stick on the handle very straight in the centre of the long sides. When I had followed the instructions accurately at last, I found that my enthusiastic licking of the decidedly pleasant gum had left very little to hold the ends in place and that the lop-sided handle wouldn't carry the weight of the basket. It was the untidiest basket in the class and I felt incompetent.

My three years in the junior classroom under Mrs Walker were equally distinct as I progressed from left to right of the room through standards two, three and four. The lessons were more clearly divided into conventional subjects because we followed a structured timetable: we chanted more complicated mathematical tables, forwards and backwards, learned spelling lists by heart, struggled with the language of the Bible. I acquired a gloomy, Old Testament picture of bearded men in strange clothing who betrayed their brothers or saw ladders reaching to heaven, or went onto a mountain to talk to God in the clouds, and a dreadful impression of dire punishment for breaking the Ten Commandments, some of which were incomprehensible and therefore menacing. And yes, Jesus miraculously healed sick people and walked on the water, and fed five thousand people with a few loaves and fishes, but warned us that we girls must be ready with trimmed lamps for some mysterious event which could happen tomorrow. Trimming the lamps made good sense; I knew how to do that so that they wouldn't smoke and blacken their chimneys.

The last lesson on Wednesday afternoons was hygiene, and I dreaded a revelation that I had some disease or would not match up to strict standards of cleanliness. Through observation and experience I became well versed in the practicalities of head lice; in standard three, on one fascinating occasion, I watched them walking on the closely cropped head of the boy in front. I learned to sew, with no clear notion of whether the needle should go from right to left, or vice versa. I learned to knit. Terrified of dropping a stitch and having to go out to Mrs Walker to have it picked up, I gripped the needles and pulled the wool tight to the point where the result was stiff and hard. To offset the cost of materials, the West Riding had a policy that the girls' completed knitting and sewing should be sold for a few pence to anyone who ordered a garment. My friend, Ivy, was a very slack knitter and she and I both made a vest for baby Harry Daniel. With the same number of stitches and rows they were incredibly different in size and I'm sure neither would be fit to wear.

Mrs Walker was a sad woman, but as her pupils we didn't realize that. Later, when I came to know and understand her better, I learned how arduous a life she had as a widow bringing up a teenage daughter and travelling from Harrogate every day in her little two-seater car. When she wasn't acting in her role as teacher she had a sense of humour and a kind heart, but in class she was intimidating. Her favoured form of discipline was ridicule, and she was merciless to those who irritated her by being slow. George Winterburn was the regular butt of her trenchant remarks. She would say, 'Well, Winterburn?' after asking a general question. His usual defence was a resigned, 'Yus', 'Naw', or 'Ah doan't knaw'. If he made a mistake she would resort to one of her favourite phrases, 'Brains! They will out!' In one memorable poetry lesson he excelled himself:

'What is the meaning of "anonymous"?'

Silence, then a few hands tentatively raised. Astonishingly, George Winterburn put up his hand.

'Yes, Winterburn?'

'Please, Miss, we doan't knaw 'oo writ it.'

Mrs Walker was momentarily silenced.

Looking back, I wonder what many village children made of the broader aspects of the curriculum, since most of them never went on holiday, never left the locality. Poetry, for example, was learned by heart, repeated by the whole class.

'I must go down to the seas again,
To the lonely sea and the sky,
And all I ask is a tall ship
And a star to steer her by.'

Of course we learned, 'Oh to be in England, now that April's there,' and, 'I wandered lonely as a cloud,' and other verses related to the countryside and flowers. We also learned well known national folk songs and hymns, to tunes practised in tonic sol fa. There were prints on the walls, including 'When did you last see your father?' and dark reproductions of famous paintings of kings and queens of England and the princes in the Tower. We had stories about children in other lands, pictures of igloos and Eskimos and of villages full of bare-footed black children. We must have had some instruction in simple current affairs, too. Newspaper pictures of Haile Selasse, who was Emperor of Abyssinia when Italy invaded it in 1936, were pinned on the wall, and, again from newspapers, official photographs when the Duke of Gloucester married Lady Alice Scott.

My favourite memory is of summer afternoons when the sunshine came through the classroom door onto standard four's desks and I read *Coral Island* by R. M. Ballantyne, lost to the classroom around me in a world of bread-fruit trees, warm seas and golden sand. The blue book had an evocative picture on the front and the text and illustrations were printed on slightly shiny paper, grimed by the hands of previous readers. To that term, also, belongs my triumphant mastery of long division – a double page of sums, all correct.

My education proceeded, too, in semi-informative conversation with some of the boys on the back rows; there weren't many girls in my class. I was usually in the back corner, with Harry Bramley (Bram'lebush), Arthur Dodson (Dogshit) and Leslie Mothersdale (Mucker) either alongside me or in the row in front. Of course, I never called any of the boys by name. On one occasion I overheard a snippet of their conversation and asked what 'balls' were, since they obviously had nothing to do with playground activity. There was muttering, nudging and covert smirking and Mucker was deputed to explain. Red-faced, he said something from which I gathered that boys had them, but I didn't hear properly and Mrs Walker didn't hear at all, and I had to wait several years before the mystery was solved.

On special occasions such as the beginning and end of term, the screen between the junior and senior classrooms was folded back for a joint assembly led by my father. We sang 'Lord behold us with thy blessing' or 'Lord dismiss us with thy blessing', which seem to have been in common use in schools at that time. There were other such occasions, though, to mark special events, the most solemn of which was Armistice Day. It is difficult, now, at eighty years' distance, with other wars remembered and wars in progress, to understand the mentality of the late 1920s and early 1930s, when the First World War was little more than a decade away. My father had been a stretcher bearer during the war. He used to say that he was one of the lucky ones because he never had to go over the top. It wasn't until I saw archive footage of the war long after he was dead, that I caught a glimpse of the reality behind those words – plucking the wounded and dying from the wire or picking them out from among their dead comrades, carrying them through the mud to the field hospital behind the lines, possibly even collecting the dead – and began to understand why he hid his feelings under a determined cheerfulness and was so passionate about the subject's duty to serve king and country. Ennobling the act was the only way to make sense of what he and those he had known had seen and gone through, and in those early years he still sincerely believed that a world fit for heroes would eventually be created, where ordinary people could live at peace under the protection of the League of Nations.

Britain was taking the lead and ruling her Empire under the guidance of God by promoting Christian values.

When we sat, wearing our penny poppies that smelt of fish glue, made for Earl Haig's Fund by the disabled servicemen themselves, fingered their black metal centres and fabric petals, and listened to his moving words in remembrance of the dead, we looked up to where the photograph of Mr Willey, headmaster in 1914, handsome, young and smiling, looked down on us. His widowed mother, deprived by war of her only son, still lived in the village. As long as my father was headmaster that photograph remained; his successor removed it, perhaps judging that it was no longer relevant in the 1950s.

It was impossible for the listening children to share his thoughts and the scenes passing before his mind's eye when he used this day of remembrance to instil into members of a young and innocent generation the pity of war, the blessing of peace, gratitude for the sacrifice made by those who 'willingly gave their lives', the virtue of remaining loyal to patriotic ideals, and the integrity, as survivors of his generation must believe it to be, of the society that was being built on the costly victory. I doubt if he questioned then the propaganda that sustained him and thousands like him. It must have been painful, when the later 1930s opened other dark probabilities, to accept increasingly that, once again, war was inevitable.

After his simple talk emphasizing the solemnity of the occasion, we stood for the two minutes' silence and then sang, with real feeling, a hymn which appeared in a generation of hymn books of all denominations:

1. I vow to thee, my country, all earthly things above,
    Entire and whole and perfect, the service of my love;
    The love that asks no question, the love that stands the test,
    That lays upon the altar the dearest and the best;
    The love that never falters, the love that pays the price,
    The love that makes undaunted the final sacrifice.

2. And there's another country I've heard of long ago,

Most dear to them that love her, most great to them that
know;
We may not count her armies, we may not see her King;
Her fortress is a faithful heart, her pride is suffering;
And soul by soul and silently her shining bounds increase,
And her ways are ways of gentleness and all her paths are
peace.

On checking the words of this hymn I discovered that it was
dated 1918, written by Sir Cecil Spring-Rice (1859-1918), a lifelong diplomat educated at Eton and Oxford, who was British
Ambassador to the United States from 1912 to 1918. No further
comment is needed.

The festive preparation for Christmas involved the whole
school. Using wallpaper samples from well-used pattern books
donated by Billy Burrell, the children made paper chains and
Japanese lanterns to hang from them and looped them from the
picture rails and from the central lamps to the corners of the
rooms. Somewhere tucked away were the folding bells and larger
decorations that came out annually, and each class heard the
Christmas story and practised well known carols. Excitement
mounted when the Christmas tree appeared in my father's
classroom, waiting for decoration. Meanwhile, my mother, a
meticulous craftswoman, had been making containers for sweets,
which my parents bought in large jars from Mrs Metcalfe. I
helped to fill them and was always sworn to secrecy. I never saw
the tree being decorated – presumably that was done after I had
gone to bed, but soon it held a named gift for every child in the
school.

At the final assembly the screen was folded back, the infants
crowded in and carols were sung. My father always talked about
the joy and meaning of Christmas and vowed he believed in
Santa Claus. His word was good enough for me against all the
murmurings of, 'It's only yer Mam and Dad'. I believed in Santa
Claus until I was nine, my last Christmas at Great Ouseburn
school. After the end of term I questioned my mother in bed one
morning, and she asked me what I really thought. Wanting her to

contradict me, I said I supposed it would be difficult for him to get down all the chimneys and, to my utter mortification, realised that I had looked a fool in front of my friends. It seemed a very lame explanation to suggest that Santa represented the spirit of Christmas; as far as I could see, my parents had deceived me and my dad had lied. We played Santa Claus for several years, but the magic of Christmas had gone. It had never been part of our celebration to give presents to each other in addition to what Santa brought: I had never learned to give, only to receive; so once the magic was explained away nothing was left but a jolly pretence. I could never bring myself to tell my children stories of Santa.

I'm glad that I could help to prepare the celebrations in school and could enjoy the other children's excitement as the gifts were handed out. When the tree was bare, the children returned to their classrooms, decorations were dismantled, and they were given their own named lanterns to take home on pieces of streamer. They rushed out at the end of the day, scarves and streamers flying. The tree was brought into our front room, placed in the bay window, and we decorated it again with our collection of baubles, tinsel, candles in clip-on holders, and home-made decorations, including butterflies made from toffee-papers, a good excuse to pick out the black, juicy liquorice toffees, or the coconut ones when my favourites had gone.

Finally, just after my tenth birthday, I left the village school to go into the preparatory class at Knaresborough Grammar School. I spent one week in the senior classroom before the grammar school term started, and I wished I could stay with the people I knew in the familiar village school, even being taught by my dad. I enjoyed his lessons; behind his superficial strictness he was good-humoured, understanding and kind. He was popular with both girls and boys, who knew just when they could take advantage a little with impunity and when to draw the line. I was told years later by more than one former classmate that the older boys regarded him as human and laughed good-humouredly behind his back, because he would go out to stoke the greenhouse fire and come back smelling of tobacco. Even so, they appreciated his teaching. George Winterburn, who lived in the village all his life and worked as a motor mechanic in the local garage, was instrumental in the success of the local gardening club, grew prize-winning flowers and vegetables, and told my dad that he owed his lifelong interest in gardening to what he had learned at school. Several people have told me over the years that nobody in the village was better liked or more respected, a delightful tribute.

CHAPTER V

The playground

My real education began in the school yard, where I had to make my way among children of my own age. It was not easy. If I am to be honest about the sense of difference which plagued me throughout my years in the village school, and even afterwards when we went back to the neighbourhood to live, I must admit that it originated not so much from the fact that my father was the headmaster as from my mother's extension to me of her own obsession with the way I should be perceived. She couldn't supervise me in the classroom and playground, but she did her best to control my responses to other children.

Understandably, I was not allowed to use and not supposed even to go into the toilet block in the girls' playground, where the boys of the infants' class used a wall with a gutter, and the cans and wooden seats were in cubicles with doors. I was expected to go back into the house at the beginning of every playtime. Of course, like the other Great Ouseburn children, I had my dinner at home, while those who lived too far away brought their own food. These constraints meant that I had to separate from my playmates and scuttle across the boys' playground to the house and back again several times a day. I doubt whether anyone else, boys or girls, gave it a thought, but I felt different because no other girl went into the older boys' yard at playtime.

I was frequently reminded that I was the schoolmaster's daughter, that I was not like the other children, and that a great deal was expected of me. I must always set an example by behaving well, not pushing myself forward when playing games, not joining in arguments, never saying anything mean to anyone.

I was not allowed to take sweets into the playground because I couldn't share them with everybody, and was not to ask for or accept sweets from other children. If I had a new dress or shoes I was not to tell anybody that it was new, because 'a lot of the children' came from homes where they didn't have many new clothes and had to wear what the other children had grown out of, and I might seem to be showing off . In some respects the strategy worked, because I became partly a conformist participant, partly an observer: I was satisfied to let others make the decisions and joined in contentedly when they had been made. With no brothers or sisters as sparring partners I didn't understand people's need for tedious and time-wasting assertiveness.

Undoubtedly, the fact that I was the headmaster's daughter made a difference, though I couldn't analyse it then. I realize, now, that the other children had their out-of-school friendship groups and that, though not actively ignored, I was rarely positively sought out in group games. Two of the older girls, who were spiteful with everyone, would occasionally plague me by pretending that I'd done something awful, point at me and say, 'Oooh, I'll tell yer dad of you!' and if I asked why they'd say, 'Fer eatin' yer father's mustard,' a euphemism for something very unpleasant, and then laugh. As a result of these pressures I was always aware of being separate, always wanting to be one of the crowd and not quite managing it.

I had been taught to speak grammatically correct English (virtually free of a northern accent, but without the long 'a', which was regarded as an unpleasant and unjustifiable southern aberration). To fit into this environment I needed a working knowledge of a new language. If someone had a bag of sweets, those begging would say, 'Gi'us a goodie,' or 'Gi'us yan,' (the old sheep-counting number one), to which, if one were not feeling generous, to which the reply would be, 'Gi'us gi'us gets nowt, please is ovver late!'

In autumn those children with fruit trees in the garden would have an apple every day, and others would beg, 'Gi'us yer core!' An article dropped in the playground might be difficult to reclaim: 'Finders, keepers; losers, weepers', and an argument would follow, ending with the object being restored to its owner. The right to take some coveted position in a game would be ensured by being the first to say, 'Bags I!' When lining up to take turns in a game the order was decided by someone shouting, 'Fuzzy', followed by 'Seggy', 'Thirdy', 'Fourthy', after which, people jostled to join the line. I was one of the jostlers.

There were rhymes to taunt people who broke playground conventions for acceptable behaviour, such as telling tales to the teacher or reporting to others something that had been said about them; even the threat to do this would elicit:

'Tell tale tit,
Yer tongue shall be split,
And all the dogs in Ouseburn
Shall have a little bit!'

People would be 'dared' to do something embarrassing and virtually impossible, such as kiss an unpopular member of the opposite sex; if they resisted being pushed into the boys' yard, the taunt would be,

'Cowardy, cowardy custard,
Eat yer father's mustard.'

There were 'mucky' rhymes to be giggled over, such as a series of date-rhymes which began in 1902 and went as far as 1910 – interestingly, coinciding with the reign of King Edward VII. I soon acquired a vague idea of what they meant. I'd be interested to know if they had been there for twenty years already and how long they survived. I can remember only two of them:

In nineteen hundred and two,
The bobbies had nothing to do,
But sit on a box
And tickle their cocks,
In nineteen hundred and two.

In nineteen hundred and six,
The king was chopping sticks,
He missed the block
And chopped his cock,
In nineteen hundred and six.

In spite of my mother's precautions, then, I soon gained knowledge it was prudent to hide, including the concept that some words were banned as 'swear words'. I imagined that some form of retribution would follow if they were uttered, but this didn't fit my rudimentary sense of logic. Why should 'bugger' be a swear word if 'beggar' wasn't? They sounded very similar. So, one day, just as we were lining up to go in from play, I said, 'Bugger!' to Ivy.

She was scandalized: '*Ooooh, you swore!*' The sun still shone and we went into school, and absolutely nothing happened; end of experiment; it's an ugly word, anyway.

I was saved from loneliness by my friendship with Ivy Benson, a good-natured, warm-hearted, companionable and popular girl, who looked on me as her best friend in the playground. What she played, I played, and we remained inseparable as long as I was at the school. She shared with me her small triumphs: 'Ah've getten me scab off,' as she showed me the healing graze. I can't remember that I reciprocated other than by being amenable to her wishes and a good listener. I've often wondered why she chose to be my friend; perhaps she had too many brothers and was a bit lonely herself.

I regarded her as the authoritative voice of public opinion. I would go home aiming to enlighten my parents: 'People are saying...'

My dad would laugh and reply, 'People, meaning Ivy?' and I would subside resentfully, or lose my temper and tell them, whether they were interested or not.

She was one of the younger members of a very large family. Her two older sisters had died of typhoid fever in their late teens when the drinking water from one of the village pumps in Little Ouseburn had been contaminated with effluent, and she was the only remaining girl. Among her older brothers were Oor Joe, Oor John, Oor Arthur, and younger than her, Oor Stan, Oor Geoff, Oor Fred, and eventually she told me excitedly that she had a new baby sister, Jean, who proved to be the last of the line. When Fred started school Ivy explained that he was a bit slow and she would have to look after him. One of the boys always told her if Fred had a problem, and once, when we were playing together, she cheerfully took disaster in her stride: 'Oor Fred's baba'd 'issen. Ah'll 'ave ter go and clean 'im oop.' Such was the lot of a girl.

Their father was a farm labourer and, although some of her older brothers were working, there must have been very little money. Even so, all the children's hair was neatly trimmed and washed regularly and they were always clean. They were never at school in torn clothing; Ivy's dresses were faded, but carefully ironed and mended. I wondered why all her finger nails were covered in white spots, the only obvious signs of chronic deficiency in her diet. I used to save my ginger biscuit for her when I had my cod liver oil, but the oil would have done her more good. In her mid-twenties, a few months before I was married, Ivy married an older man from Little Ouseburn who had remained single for many years after his fiancée died.

She had an apt turn of phrase. On Mrs Walker's first day, Ivy saw her before I did. When I went across to the playground that morning, she said excitedly: ' 'Ave yer seen t'new teacher? She's as far roond as that there tree!' pointing to the aged ash tree in the field. When I saw her I was inclined to agree.

Often Ivy would relate the ongoing saga of after-school life in Little Ouseburn, where there were plenty of other children as well as the Bensons. I envied her the exciting evenings when all the local children played in Mr Clough's field or the village street. Regularly, in summer, there were tramps in the locality, some of them itinerant labourers looking for casual seasonal work and well known to the farmers, who would give them cast-offs and let them sleep in the buildings while they were working on the farm. They could be seen plodding along the high road, with their bearded, weathered faces, dirty trousers, ragged coats tied with binder twine, and worn boots, their few belongings tied up in a dirty cloth and slotted onto a stout stick carried over one shoulder. These men attracted the derision of the pack of village children, and I often heard stories of 'oard fellas': 'When we wo' playin' oot last neet, there were an oard fella, so we called 'im an'e run us.' They lived life recklessly in Little Ouseburn, and how I wished I could join them!

In many respects the playgrounds were self-regulating communities, the true cultural centre of school life in its social aspects. There was no overt rivalry or tendency to form cliques around certain strong personalities; people played whatever game the majority were playing, or broke into smaller groups to chat together or play something different. Anybody being too assertive or boastful was told, 'Yer only cleverin' off!' I wonder how far this easy assumption of equality and co-operation reflected the agricultural society in which these children lived, where it was the key to successful adult working practice, where families tended to be large, social aspirations were virtually unknown, and only the few people of a different social class were much better off than their neighbours. It was a playground community into which I could slip unobtrusively and be accepted by being quiet and agreeable.

The older boys had only a passing interest in organising games; they seemed to race about, kick a ball, or tumble in friendly heaps in their own playground; the little boys in the girls' playground ran around on the fringes of the girls' play. This had seasonal rhythms which slotted into the special highlights of marbles, whip and top, and conkers, played throughout the school. Sometimes skipping would be the main activity and we were allowed to bring out the long, thick ropes supplied for P.E., in addition to our own small skipping ropes. Sometimes we just played 'waves', running in and out of the group who were jumping over the waving rope. Occasionally we played high jumps, the younger ones and poor jumpers being eliminated until the seniors competed to jump the highest. A few of the older girls adopted a roll which enabled them to jump almost their own height. The most popular choice was communal skipping. Two people would 'bag' the right to 'twined' the rope and the others would jump in and out. Finally, someone would call for 'peppers' and we would chant, 'Pitch, patch, pepper!' and try to keep up with the increasing speed. As an alternative we played French skipping, where the rope was doubled and moved in two directions. It was much harder to jump in and out of the resulting loop while keeping up the faster pace, but a satisfying skill, and most of us became adept.

Ball games took their turn. A particular favourite played by bouncing the ball against a wall had six stages of increasing difficulty: six plain bounces and catches, then five times under a raised leg, four times thrown from behind through open legs, three times between the legs with one's back to the wall, twice thrown high on the wall and once with the ball thrown round one's back to bounce on the wall. The reward for total success in catching the ball was another turn, but anyone who made a mistake dropped out. This was one game I could enjoy by myself when everyone else had gone home.

In hot weather we sometimes sat in the shade and played families, choosing characters to act the parts of strident mother and father and a host of quarrelsome, disobedient children who always answered back, were shouted at and given a good smacking. I didn't like this game, which didn't represent life as I knew it, but of course I wasn't chosen as one of the parents and I didn't get shouted at or smacked. Boring, but it probably parodied experience in some families; it has its more sophisticated television equivalent in *Eastenders* and *Coronation Street*.

When we needed to choose someone to be 'it' we stood in a ring and someone 'bagged' the right to 'call'. We had two rhymes. The simpler and quicker was, 'Boy scout, walk out;' the second was 'Spuds', in which all those playing put up their fists and the caller tapped one fist after another, chanting, 'One potato, two potato, three potato, four, five potato, six potato, seven potato, more.' The fist on which 'more' was tapped went behind one's back until only one remained.

We played several versions of 'tig': the plain version, where anyone caught becomes 'it', was routinely played by small groups, but 'chain tig' could involve all the girls; if caught, you joined the chain until it stretched right across the yard and took in the stragglers. We had another version called 'sticky', where anyone caught became sticky and was imprisoned against the top wall unless freed by someone who eluded the person who was 'it' and could neutralize the stickiness. With a skilful catcher one game could last through the whole of dinner-time play without reaching a conclusion, as the line of those who were sticky grew or diminished against the wall.

Occasionally we played *What time is it, Mr Wolf?* Where one person, the wolf, stood against the wall that divided the playgrounds, hiding her eyes, and all the others tiptoed towards her shouting the question, until she replied, 'One o'clock', or some other hour in random order and turned round sharply. Anyone seen moving must drop out. The aim was for someone to touch her before she shouted 'Dinner time!' and chased the remaining players back to the fence, hoping to catch the next 'wolf'.

There were singing games involving large groups of girls. A favourite was *The rain, the rain*, where one player was pushed, laughing, into the centre of a circle of singers, who then whispered an agreed name to be shouted as they walked round holding hands and singing:

The rain, the rain, the rain is high, the rain comes scattering from the sky,
Dulcie Barlow says she'll die, if she doesn't get a boy with a bonny blue eye.
Skiddy Whitwell says he loves her; all the boys are fighting for her,
Let the boys say what they will, *Skiddy Whitwell* loves her still.
He huddles her, he cuddles her, he sits her on his knee,
He says, 'My pretty darling, what will you have for tea?'
'A china cup and saucer, a guinea gold ring,
And a plate to put the pudding on, ding, dong, ding.'

The fun lay in shouting the name of an unlikely partner and laughing at the shrieks of denial from the victim before the singing continued.

Another regular game was *The farmer wants a wife*, which also started with one person in the centre of the ring, to be joined by others chosen in turn, while those in the circle sang:

The farmer wants a wife; the farmer wants a wife,

Chorus: ee-aye, ee-aye the farmer wants a wife.
The wife wants a child; the wife wants a child,
Chorus (child).
The child wants a nurse; the child wants a nurse,
Chorus (nurse).
The nurse wants a cat; the nurse wants a cat,
Chorus (cat).
The cat wants a dog; the cat wants a dog,
Chorus (dog).
The dog wants a bone; the dog wants a bone,
Chorus (bone).
We all pat the bone; we all pat the bone,
Chorus: ee-aye, ee-aye; we all pat the bone.

As this was sung those now in the middle patted the unfortunate bone on the back and returned to the ring, leaving the bone to be the next farmer:
The bone stands alone; the bone stands alone,
Chorus: ee-aye, ee-aye, the bone stands alone.

Another favourite was *Run through, shall 'e go*. As many people as wished to play held hands to form a chain. The leader stood near the wall and pressed a raised arm against it, making a space to run through. As we repeatedly sang, 'Run through, shall 'e go, fire and shot; the one who is last is sure to be got,' we ran through the space, each in turn being forced to cross arms at the other side. Finally, when we all had our arms crossed, the leader joined the last person and we danced round in a circle singing the tune, turning first one way and then the other. Finally, the leader broke the circle, re-formed the arch and we reversed the process until all our arms were uncrossed, when the next person in line became the leader.

A simple and popular game was one where the person who was 'it' sauntered round the outside of the standing circle and, after several feints, dropped a handkerchief unobtrusively behind another girl, hoping to prevent her from realizing immediately and so gain a start in the race round the circle to occupy her space and leave her with the handkerchief. Those standing in the circle clapped until the victim picked up the handkerchief and then shouted in support of their favoured contestant.

Occasionally, we played a version of *Oranges and Lemons* where the person who was running through the arch as the chopper fell was asked to whisper a choice, such as 'buttercups or daisies', 'apples or oranges', and to line up behind the arch-maker who represented the item chosen. The longest line won.

Four distinctive dates were celebrated in the school yard. Shrove Tuesday, Pancake Day, was the time to play 'shuttlecock and battledore'. The battledore was a flat, plywood bat, shaped like a table tennis bat, and the shuttlecock was like a badminton feather. The game was to hit the feather repeatedly into the air and catch it on the bat, more difficult than it would appear because the bat was solid and the shuttlecock unpredictable, especially if there was a breeze. You could have as many pancakes as times you hit it successfully. Comparatively few people had their own sets, but everyone shared and it was good fun.

In a society where possessions were few and pleasures were simple, April Fool's Day was eagerly anticipated and enthusiastically celebrated. The excitement of playing tricks on the constantly wary dominated the morning until the moment after twelve o'clock when the trickster became the fool. Some tricks were relatively simple, such as telling someone that a shoelace was undone or they had a hole in their sock, or that there was a money spider on their back, but only the constantly alert avoided the more casually spoken traps. Even in the classroom you might be told that you'd ink on your face or you'd dropped your hanky, and the least twitch of reaction made you the fool. The boys always hoped to catch my dad, often telling him that there was someone at the door who wanted to see him, and occasionally he would please them by falling for the old ploy.

An equivalent version, May Gosling, celebrated on the first of May, was new to my father when he came to Great Ouseburn School. Iona And Peter Opie, in *The Lore and Language of Schoolchildren* (Oxford, Clarendon Press, 1959), p. 256, write that children attempt to make 'May Goslings' in only a small part of the country, at Workington in West Cumberland and to the east of the county at Penrith, at Topcliffe, and throughout the area around Thirsk in the North Riding of Yorkshire, eastward toward Scarborough and south to York. Though in the West Riding, Great Ouseburn was only a mile from the North Riding, the River Ure being the boundary. The Ouseburn people regarded themselves as distinct from 'them ovver't watter', but this game respected no boundaries. The two occasions were highlights of the spring and we enjoyed the second opportunity for a morning's fun and laughter.

The fourth celebration, much less pleasant, has also been recorded by the Opies (pp. 263-266, distribution map, p. 265). It commemorated the Restoration of Charles II on 29 May, 1660, which was then declared by Act of Parliament a day of annual thanksgiving. It perpetuated the story that, after Boscobel, he hid from his enemies in an oak tree. Everybody had to wear a piece of 'royal oak', and we went up and down the playground chanting, 'The twenty-ninth of May is Royal Oak Day. If we don't get a holiday we'll all run away.' Some of the boys, even the little ones, ran around with stinging nettles and stung the bare legs of anyone not wearing the oak. Both boys and girls had bare legs, because the boys wore short trousers and the girls wore dresses or skirts.

As in similar districts throughout England, this ferocious ritual was a legacy of the bitterness engendered by the Civil War, when men of property and influence in Great and Little Ouseburn had been on opposite sides, and families known to support the king's cause, particularly strong in Little Ouseburn, had been severely penalized under the Commonwealth. Still, in the 1920s and 1930s, there was an echo of distrust between the two villages. The children, now together in one school, mixed happily, but a few older people would not go to an event in the other village.

In autumn, we raided the horse chestnut trees for potential winners, and played 'conkers'. Both school yards were strewn with fragments of the defeated, and a strong specimen that had proved itself in battle was cherished. I always kept my undefeated one on its string in my toy drawer for a while, to gloat over it and admire its colour and smoothness. Although the craze didn't last long, boys and girls played with others they rarely spoke to; it was a good spectator sport and created a great deal of friendly rivalry, laughter and cheering.

The children never dawdled to school on frosty days. In both playgrounds the first to arrive, particularly those with suitable boots, made a long, slippery slide; then we all waited in a line taking turns to run as fast as possible to begin the slide at speed, either standing or doing, 'little man', that is, gradually crouching down in motion to end the slide squatting, if you didn't fall on your bottom. I always went into the playground early on frosty mornings. Newcomers would shout, 'Is it slape?' (slippery) and rush to join the waiting line. Nobody wearing wellingtons was allowed to play, because they blunted the slide. On sunny days the slide in the girls' playground would have melted by afternoon playtime, but it could be refreshed the next day if the frost returned. Vale of York cloudy highs were just as common then, and the same slide could last for days and build up a strong, glassy surface. Nothing was more exhilarating than keen, frosty air tingling the nostrils and chilling deep in the lungs and the triumph of fast movement under perfect control. Snowy weather has left fewer memories; there was some snowballing, but we were not allowed to get thoroughly wet; Mr Smith cleared paths through the yards and spread ashes on them. Playtimes then were spent indoors, keeping warm.

Fine, warm, sunny afternoons were particularly memorable. Instead of going back into school after playtime, the boys went into Jacksons' field to play cricket and the junior and senior girls stayed in the yard for country dancing, taught by Miss Dawson. We learned *Gathering Peascods* and *Sellenger's Round* among others. We danced to records played on a wind-up gramophone set on a carefully levelled table. Every few minutes it would slow down and someone had to dash across and wind it up again before it stopped completely, so that we could get back to speed. It made an exciting change to have longer out of doors in the sunshine, because very little time was devoted to formal games and 'drill', as physical education was called. I have only the vaguest memory of going out into the playground to form lines and jump, bend and stretch to order. On beautiful days we had extended playtimes; the two women stood chatting and watching from the cloakroom window and my dad went into the house for a cup of tea and a cigarette – or two.

CHAPTER VI

Village life: memorable people

The living room window was my open eye to village life. As a small child I was held up to look over the net half-curtain that shrouded the lower panes; later, I just watched the passers-by: people on bicycles, horses and carts with hay, corn stooks, turnips, sugar beet, 'worzels', potatoes, the water cart rumbling down to the slipway by the fish-pond bridge, Percy Cuthbert with his barrow and tools, Mrs Metcalfe and Aunt Edie hurrying along the footpath to each other's doors. There were motor vehicles, too, particularly delivery vans, and when the first tractors came to the village, I ran out to look as soon as I heard one.

One person survives only as a wraith in memory, an afternoon figure, a spidery caricature moving across the field of vision from left to right. Old Miss Dalby: very tiny, very thin, always in black – hat with a half-veil, lacy shawl, skirt, spindly, stockinged legs, old-fashioned buttoned boots, gloves – a covered wicker basket over her arm; strange, hopping walk, lifting her feet high, prancing down the footpath. She made me shiver, being so black and wizened and small, but what was she really like? What was her life? She lived in Branton, but where was she going? Why the basket? Visiting someone? No answers, just a strange, dark figure I can't remember meeting in the street; she merely passed by.

Often when people walked or cycled past I would ask who they were, and I recognized more people than I ever spoke to. I would probably be eight or nine when I noticed two people in their teens, whom I didn't recognize, leaning their bikes against

Mrs Metcalfe's wall. In reply to my query, my mother said they were Barbara and Donald Stead, who had recently come to live in the village. I thought, 'Barbara Stead, Donald Stead, Stead, Stead. What a lovely name!' I loved words, and there was a quietness and stability in the sound which appealed to me; I can't remember being attracted to any other name as distinct from its owner. I wasn't predisposed to favour the man I eventually married because of his surname; as students we were always on first-name terms and it was a while before I knew it; but, when I came to realize it would be my name for most of my life, I was intrigued by the memory – a very clear visualization of the image, the query, and my meditative response.

Dickie Kettlewell, the chimney sweep, small and thin, very upright, pedalled up and down the street, his face black-streaked and sooty, his rods and brushes tied to the crossbar of his old 'sit up and beg' bike, the round, bristled ends projecting behind. His children, Amy, Sarah, Ernest and Jack were all at school, thin children with frizzy hair, scrubbed red cheeks and flaky skin. Sarah was my contemporary, pleasant and friendly. Dickie was always very busy in spring and autumn, the traditional cleaning seasons, and filled in the rest of the year with casual labouring work. He didn't come to our house because Mr Smith lent us his set of brushes. Chimney-sweeping day was very exciting: carpet up, curtains down, floors covered with old sheets and one pushed close to the fireplace to collect the soot for the back-yard bin. I was given the 'important' task of watching to see when the brush popped out of the top of the chimney. Our chimneys were tall and needed all the rods. It was a filthy job and the fine soot lingered, so occasionally, to postpone it, my dad would set the accumulated soot on fire by putting an Imp up the chimney. These small blocks, when set alight, jumped into the chimney stack, burned fiercely, and a pall of smoke and sparking, red-hot patches of burning soot emerged spectacularly from the chimney pot. It was anti-social to set a chimney on fire deliberately, but Imps were on the market and it was common practice. After all, accidents will happen in the months of bright winter fires and burning logs; he always chose a dark evening!

The village had its elite. Sometimes Miss Thompson would ride by in her large, chauffeur-driven car, her elaborate pile of grey hair surmounted by an elegant hat with a veil, or Captain and Mrs Tunstill from Moat Hall would drive past in a more fashionable model, her Pekinese dogs yapping at the back windows as eagerly as they yapped at the gates when we were passing on foot. The captain, a war veteran, was the first person I knew who took advantage of the fatal effect of putting a tube from the exhaust pipe into a car, closing the garage doors, sitting in the driver's seat and turning on the engine. His widow lived alone in the large house for several years after his death and continued to be active in village life, though she spent the winters in Italy. She sometimes called on my mother and I was fascinated by her gracious manner. Her well powdered face with its social smile was set on a short neck above her enormous but well-controlled bust, which appeared to be one flesh and bore no relation to the size of her hips and legs.

Even in such a small village we were able to buy fish fresh from the market in Grimsby. On Tuesdays and Thursdays Mr Truby called. Like the carrier, Mr Jennison, he went to Cattal station early in the morning and collected his delivery from the train. He had a horse and cart, the horse with a nosebag and the cart carrying as much variety of fish as would be found in any town of the day or any modern supermarket. Having already served Whixley and Little Ouseburn, he came mid-morning, his hand-bell announcing his arrival. The neighbourhood cats knew the sound and materialized to follow his cart and snatch a fish-head or some oily guts as he threw them the trimmings.

He was short, red-cheeked and stocky, with a handle-bar moustache, and wore very thick boots; I was told he had been born without toes. He came clumping up the steps, splay-footed, and rang the doorbell.

'I've got cod, haddock, some nice thick plaice, lemon sole, halibut, Scarborough woof, whiting, silver hake, kippers, bloaters, some lovely fresh herrings, mackerel, and there's some really good crabs today.'

We usually had white fish and one other choice. I was impressed with his ability to select herrings with hard roes, which

I enjoyed more than the bony fish itself. My mother was careful about buying crabs because they were pre-cooked, but, when we had this treat, I helped to prepare it. She would remove the 'devil's fingers' and scoop out the soft, yellow meat. Then she would break the claws with a flat iron, so that we could pick out the white flesh and mix it with the other before seasoning and potting the mixture in a small basin, topping it with melted butter, and putting it away until tea-time under a fine wire mesh cover on the stone slab in the cool pantry to keep the flies away. We often had kippers for tea. My mother and I had ours cooked in the frying pan, kept moist by an inverted plate, but my dad liked to cook his own over the fire on a gridiron. He used to boast that nobody else could eat a kipper as neatly as he could, a challenge which resulted in my making a pretty good attempt. For neither of us did the process involve a knife and fork; fingers and a piece of bread and butter did a far better job; the backbone and loose bones could be lifted aside, the oil on the plate and kipper skin could be mopped up cleanly, and fingers could be licked to enjoy the last of the keen, smoky flavour. I confess that this would still be my preferred method. When faced with a kipper for breakfast as a student living in a hostel and compelled by convention to use a knife and fork, the pleasure of the experience was lost in embarrassing ineptitude.

Other trades-people came through the village several times a week: from Boroughbridge, Miss Morten bringing cakes, pastries and Hovis bread, and Mr Walton bringing fruit; from Knaresborough once a fortnight, the hardware man with an adapted van, carrying a rack of pans, kettles and other household goods. Since the fire was most people's source of heat for cooking, pans and kettles wore out quickly. The butcher came on Tuesdays and Fridays, from Boroughbridge in the early days and then from Little Ouseburn when Willie Barrit set up in business there.

Dr Benson, who held his surgery in his house opposite the church, would emerge briskly from his car, clad in dignity and a slightly shabby suit and carrying his worn brown leather bag. His superior manner and army officer's accent separated him from ordinary folk, and he attracted the respect and projected the authority of his profession. Dr Benson and my father had served together during the war, when he had been the officer in charge of the medical unit to which my father was attached as a sergeant stretcher-bearer; so there was always good feeling between them. When, at the age of three, I had serious tonsillitis which almost turned to pneumonia, I became familiar with him, but never comfortable, because he had a loud voice and would hold down my tongue with one of the best teaspoons from the sideboard in the front room, where I was lying on the sofa in front of the fire, and make me say, 'Aah'.

Tragically, the Bensons' sons were two of the only three village men killed in the Second World War. The elder, Noel, a Spitfire pilot, died in the Battle of Britain; Brian, an army captain, was killed in the last week of fighting. Their daughter, Margaret, a small, thin girl, was two years older than me and privately educated. Immaculately dressed in black peaked riding-hat, black jacket and white jodhpurs, upright and elegant, long fair pigtail down the centre of her back, she exercised her pony gently through the village and round the back lanes, awaking in me an intense longing for a horse; I never accepted that we couldn't have one when there was Jacksons' field alongside the school. She was quaintly formal, but charming when we exchanged pleasantries, never worked, never married, lived with her parents until they both died, when she sold the house and left the village.

Not everybody could afford the fee for a doctor's visit, but Nurse Mitchell was always available. The village Nursing Association, a money-raising organization, paid the salary of a fully trained nurse, qualified as a midwife, to serve anyone in need in the village free of charge. My parents contributed generously and, in the early years, they made cane-work trays, tables and chairs for sale at the annual bazaar. The trays were very popular and my father cut out and varnished plywood bases and pierced them with holes around the edges so that, as part of their handwork lessons, the older children could weave soaked cane to form the sides and insert decorative beads at each end. The child's chair my parents made for me survived, much worn, into the next generation of the family.

There was a personal reason for their commitment. When I was born in the September after they came to live in the village, my mother's labour lasted from Monday until Wednesday, under Nurse Mitchell's care and Dr Benson's supervision. Today, with her small pelvis, she would have a Caesarean section, but then nature took its painful course to the final point where Dr Benson asked my father if they should save the mother or the child, because it was unlikely they could save both. He was told to save the mother. I understand that, when the baby finally arrived, weak, but able to take her first breath, my mother's needs came first, and my father's sister, Auntie Connie, who had been keeping my mother company and running the household, took the small, purplish scrap, wrapped her in warm flannel and sat by the fire with her, gently comforting and soothing her, and she lived. I can well understand the intensity of their concern for me, particularly as they were warned that in no circumstances must they have any more children. My mother, more than my father, was by nature possessive, and I became the centre of her life. He adored his wife and daughter, so nearly lost to him, and both were over-protective of me. Whatever my frustrations, though, I always knew that I was loved.

My mother had a special affection for Nurse Mitchell, and I sensed the bond. When she visited the Clarksons I would see her getting out of her car, wearing her blue uniform, with white starched collar, white apron and nurse's veil. Carrying her bag, she would walk elegantly up to their door, and my mother would say warmly, 'There's Auntie Nurse.' She was a pretty woman, well made up, with fair, fluffy hair peeping from under the veil and a gentle voice and ready smile, her distinctive accent owing nothing to the locality and something to her status. The back seat of her car was always occupied by Folly, her curly-haired golden Labrador.

She was a widow with one daughter, Margaret, also a nurse, who lived and worked in Harrogate and often visited her. Occasionally, we were invited to have afternoon tea at the house between the *Three Horse Shoes* and the Village Institute, also known as the Reading Room, where she lodged with her close friends, Mr and Mrs Townend. I loved to go there, more because of Folly and the cakes than because of Auntie Nurse. I was very impressed on one occasion when she said she was convinced that animals have souls and Folly would be waiting for her in heaven; if it wasn't so, she didn't want to go. I was sure she must be right about dogs going to heaven, because Folly was far too gentle and loving not to deserve a place there.

Tusie, our Yorkshire terrier, was badly scalded at the age of six. A full kettle of newly boiled water slipped off its stand on the hearth and the dog happened to be eating near it. Auntie Nurse treated her wounds and bandaged her and came every day for several weeks until her back and side were properly healed. Tusie would certainly have died without this careful nursing. I used to stand by her as she was working on the dressings, her hands dexterous inside the rubber gloves, and gaze anxiously at the slowly healing raw flesh. She smelt attractively of perfume and powder, tempered by the smell of cigarettes, and I admired the delicate rouge and lipstick that gave her face the quality of a china doll in spite of the incipient wrinkles. I thought she was very beautiful. Nobody then queried the health and safety aspects of her carrying Folly round on the back seat of her car and treating a dog along with her human patients as part of her rounds.

CHAPTER VII

Village life: special events

The village community was much livelier than our semi-isolated position allowed me to experience. Indoor events took place in the Barn Hall, a large building in the vicarage grounds with its door opening into Church Lane. In the 1930s, the vicarage was still an imposing establishment with stable block and a yard spacious enough for carriages and horses, although only Mr and Mrs Laidman lived there. Like most country vicarages built when many vicars were younger sons of the gentry, it had been expected to accommodate visiting church dignitaries and their servants, as well as to house the vicar's family and staff. Until the village was extended to meet the needs of commuting professionals, the Barn Hall was the only building in the lane apart from the cart sheds belonging to Prospect Farm. The vicarage has now been greatly reduced in size and the converted barn demolished, with the loss of part of the village heritage. I have always assumed that it was originally a tithe-barn associated with the church, but, by the 1920s, it had been equipped with a stage, a back-stage area, chairs, tables and simple catering facilities, and served for many years as the village hall, where regular whist drives and dances took place and productions by the local dramatic and choral societies were performed.

These societies drew on talent from the surrounding villages. The choral society, of which Miss Dawson was a keen member, was trained by a Green Hammerton man and met in the school on Friday evenings during term time. As I was being put to bed, his soft-topped, two-seater car would arrive in the boys' playground and most other members would come on foot. I would sneak a look through the bedroom window as the singers went into school, climb into bed again, and fall asleep to their singing.

A wealthy Whixley woman, Miss Kitty Rhodes, daughter of a retired army colonel, was an accomplished singer with an eye for costume and a taste for comedy, pantomime and light opera. She produced and took the lead in most neighbourhood theatrical performances, and we attended all her productions when I was old enough. Exceptionally, *Merrie England* was performed in the grounds of Moat Hall. I must have been very young, but I can remember being taken to it and being intrigued by the costumes and the singing. My mother sang *The Yeomen of England* for weeks afterwards, together with a chorus, *Oh 'tis folly to run away from love*, but she substituted 'golly' for 'love', in honour of my golliwog and to avoid expressing an unwelcome sentiment. As far as I was concerned, the three-times repeated, 'Oh, 'tis folly' referred to Auntie Nurse's dog.

The field behind and below Starra Cottage was the cricket field, where outdoor community events were held. It had been left for the use of the village on condition that the cricket pitch would always be maintained, an undertaking ignored during the Second World War, when most centuries-old meadows in the locality were ploughed up by order of the government to grow essential food crops. The section of its back hedge adjoining a small copse consisted of bramble bushes at least eight feet high, laden with huge, juicy fruit in early September, particularly if you used a walking stick to hook down the high branches. In autumn, too, for those out early to pick them, button mushrooms erupted across the field every morning, glistening with dew. We sometimes went down before breakfast to see what we could gather. They matured during the day, and many open-cupped ones, picked in the afternoon, had large grubs actively tunnelling in their thick caps. My dad would eat them, grubs and all, fried with bacon, arguing that all they'd eaten was mushroom, so it didn't matter. He just smiled when I said that didn't make them mushroom, picked out the juicy corpses and arranged them on the edge of my plate.

The local villages had their own cricket league and the field was used regularly throughout the summer season for Saturday matches. Team members in whites would pass by our window, each carrying his bat, white cricket boots slung over one shoulder by their laces, and supporters would gather as the opponents came in from the other villages. The pitch was immaculate, cut with a hand mower and rolled smooth and level. During the rest of the week the area of play was protected by a moveable fence, and the field was grazed by working horses. There was no pavilion.

The big outdoor events held in the cricket field were the highlights of the year. Local shows took place throughout the neighbourhood during high summer, and Great Ouseburn Agricultural and Horticultural Show was always held on August Bank Holiday Monday. My father was on the committee and exhibited regularly in the horticultural section; he regarded it as important publicity for the school. Early in the morning the exhibits were set out in the big marquee which had been put up the previous day, and I used to go with him to watch him arrange his six superb sweet peas in a tall glass vase, and roses and pansies at the peak of perfection in green-baize-covered wooden boxes with a hole for each exhibit, to display the bloom to perfection and hide its jar of water below. His pods of peas and beans and whatever other vegetables were good enough on the day were arranged more simply on large plates on the bench. I was fascinated to watch other exhibitors mounting their displays and enjoyed breathing the mixed perfumes and smells as the marquee was filled and the grass became bruised with treading. The Women's Institute members showed cakes, pickles, jams and jellies, flower arrangements, art work and handicrafts and the farmers' wives among their number exhibited eggs and butter. Cages of rabbits, ferrets and different breeds of poultry, too, were sheltered in the marquee. All these classes were judged later in the morning and, at two o'clock, the show was opened to the public. There was a rush to see which competitors had done well, and my dad always won some prizes.

Cattle and cart horses were led round the ring and judged, and there were pens of sheep and pigs, a parade by the York and

Ainsty Hunt, displays of country dancing, races for children, comic ones such as sack races and an obstacle race, a tug of war for the men, lucky dips and bobbing for apples in a bucket of water. The refreshment tent was the social centre, with everything home-made, and plenty of chairs and tables; most children didn't linger there very long, but chased around the field and sampled all the activities. True to the desired public image, I was expected to stay around in seemly manner with my mother most of the time, but I was allowed to join in the races for my age group. If it rained, as it did only too readily at the beginning of August, some outdoor events would be abandoned, but farming people are a hardy lot, philosophical about the vagaries of the climate and accustomed to its cruel tricks; takings at the gate would be down and visitors would plod round the field in wellies and stout rainwear, but there was always next year – or so it seemed.

Late September was the time for an annual event unique to Great Ouseburn: the final performance of the season in the cricket field by Barrett's Circus, before it settled in for the winter at Low Farm, Little Ouseburn, down near the river, off the road to Thorpe Underwoods.

To me as a child the circus was sheer magic. The Big Top was erected and benches for the spectators were arranged round the ring. Clowns chased each other and played tricks, elephants or lions obediently stepped onto raised platforms to pose like statues, bare-back riders performed acrobatics around the ring, dogs pushed carts, trapeze artists swung high, and Mr Barrett, the ring-master, stood in the centre, wearing a top hat and tails, cracking his whip and introducing the acts with a flourish.

George Barrett, the only son of a wealthy Huddersfield mill owner, had a passion for the circus and, for many years, the means to make a name for his show and eventually subsidize his losses. The circus went on the road throughout the country during the summer season. When it came back to Ouseburn, the Barretts, with a small crew, settled in for the winter, to repair equipment, train new acts and rest from travelling. Some performers would take winter jobs elsewhere and a few local boys gave casual help until the whole outfit reassembled and took to the road again in the spring.

During still, dark, winter nights we could hear lions roaring, elephants trumpeting and other animal noises, but the most exciting thing was to see Simla, the old female elephant ('Similar', in my mind), walking up the village. Wallace Parker had temporary work as an assistant keeper, and one of his duties was to exercise Simla, leading her through the village and along the back lanes. She would come up the road from Little Ouseburn, trunk swinging, ready to snatch a sugar beet from the roadside pile waiting to be taken to the factory in York, or pick up a crushed turnip dropped from a cart. When my dad saw her coming, he would lift me up at the front gate to hold out a carrot, and Simla would turn aside from her stolid, soft-padded progress up the street, grasp it with the sensitive end of her trunk and transfer it to her mouth. She had a twinkle in her mischievous little eyes and always seemed to be smiling, but she could be obstreperous; I was kept on the footpath if we passed her on our walk. My father's little jingle about 'Barrett's bloomin' elephant' who 'wouldn't do the stuff' was part of the rocking-chair repertoire, and it was never strange to me that an elephant should be a regular sight in the village street in winter time, any more than that there should be cartloads of turnips.

For the Barretts, our neighbourhood was home. When they were approaching retirement, they bought Abbayville in Upper Dunsforth, but Mr Barrett still dabbled with circus life and surrounded himself with circus people, some of them rogues. As his resources dwindled and his personal involvement virtually ceased, they sold Abbayville and lived in Hill Top House. The circus families with whom they were still friendly were involved mainly in providing acts for other outfits, but used to overwinter with their caravans and equipment in the field across from the house. The Barrett's son, Norman, who had trained as a ring-master, left home to work for Billy Smart's Circus, and appeared regularly on television in the early days when circus performances were still broadcast[1]. In his seventies Mr Barrett suffered from dementia, but he still loved to train poodles. He used to exercise them, walking on their hind legs and pulling little carts, in the village street. His wife, who had taken charge of the box office when they were working, was many years younger, delightfully friendly and kind. When he died, she sold the property and went to live near Norman and his family.

A special village celebration took place in May, 1935 to mark the Silver Jubilee of King George V and Queen Mary. My father wanted to make sure that the children understood the significance of the event, particularly as the king and queen were to visit the locality as part of their nationwide tour and would drive through Great Ouseburn. He was given a generous allowance of flags by the West Riding County Council, and I enjoyed helping to unpack the large cardboard container. Some had the royal coat of arms and others the Prince of Wales' feathers, and there were several splendid Union Jacks. Most were plain triangular pennants in red, white and blue. As the weather was good, the older children were able to lay them out in the boys' yard and fix them to long tapes. My father got hold of some tall, stout poles, and the flags were hoisted high across the front of the school railings, from the gate to the sycamore tree.

On the afternoon of the royal visit, the whole school trooped down to the road and stood alongside the front of the school to see the king and queen. Mrs Metcalfe and the other local people were out as well, standing on the footpath, and eventually the limousine came slowly up the road. King George was wearing full dress uniform and Queen Mary was in a light, pastel-coloured outfit with one of her characteristic matching close-fitting hats. They looked just like their photographs. The king waved to the group on the pavement and the queen, who was on our side of the car, waved to us and smiled; we waved our small Union Jacks on their sticks, and cheered. I was filled with deep joy, as if

---

[1] His name appeared in the New Year Honours List at the end of 2009, for his services to entertainment as a ringmaster.

something personal had passed between us. No other glimpse of royalty has matched that experience.

Billy Burrell made a maypole with a disk at the top holding red, white and blue braids, so that the children could perform at the main village celebration. For practice purposes it was fixed in the top drain of the girls' playground; the piano was wheeled out into the yard, and Elsie Metcalfe came to play the tunes. I was one of the team of boys and girls with some aptitude for dancing the complicated steps, who were taught by Miss Dawson to weave the beautiful traditional patterns of the maypole dances.

I've no idea how the piano was taken down to the cricket field and I can't remember the other activities of the afternoon, but taking part in that display of maypole dancing was one of the highlights of my childhood. We skipped, in couples, from the cricket field gate into the area round the maypole to the tune of *Come, lasses and lads*, ending the dance at our own ribbon. Learning the movements had been difficult and we'd tangled braids and made lop-sided patterns on the way, but Miss Dawson had been a patient teacher; we got it right; the shapes and colours were immaculate. We danced the steps to un-plait the ribbons, rewind them evenly on the pole, re-form our couples; then we danced out to enthusiastic applause.

The king died the following year and King Edward VIII abdicated before his coronation. When King George VI and Queen Elizabeth were crowned in 1937 we put up the bunting again, but there was no repetition of the maypole dancing, no royal visit, and it was a cold, wet day.

CHAPTER VIII

Out and about

The working village I knew by observation in the 1920s and early 1930s had been greatly affected by the events of 1919. Lord Knaresborough, granted an hereditary title by King Edward VII, who had been a guest at Kirby Hall on several occasions, broke up the estate after his only son was killed during the last few days of the First World War. The main hall was demolished, leaving only the servants' quarters, a substantial separate house. The building and the surrounding park and woodland were sold to Mr Penty, who felled some of the trees and sold the timber to cover the cost of his purchase. Some farms, also, were sold; others were still tenanted. Much of the park between the house and the road remained as grazing land.

These were recent events when my parents moved to Great Ouseburn and the village retained much of the working practice of an estate village tied to a wealthy landowner. Farming was labour-intensive: many farm labourers worked for the larger farms, but the West Riding was already setting up small-holdings, viable for a family. There was a niche for far-sighted men with a bit of capital, such as Harry Knowles, whose father now owned the Kirby estate's former home farm. When he married Agnes Smith he invested in a threshing machine and developed a business in Branton Green 'thrashing' corn over the autumn and winter as farmers needed his services.

The simple, farming way of life was still dependent on shire horses for ploughing, harrowing, pulling seed drills and machines for cutting hay and corn, binding the wheat, barley and oats, and for pulling carts of various types. Headlands and the weeds in

111

permanent grazing land were cut by men with scythes. Skill with the scythe was an essential attribute of the farm labourer, the best of them, like Wilf Richardson's father, able to cut grass more closely and evenly than a machine could. Teams of men worked in a line planting potato sets, hoeing turnips and sugar beet to thin the rows and eliminate weeds. The hay was turned with hay forks with specially curved tines; then piled loosely into haycocks for carting to the farm yard and making into thatched stacks. These were sometimes built in field corners, where there was less chance of damage if one should overheat. They provided first-class accommodation for rats and mice.

The Vale of York, unlike the Wolds of the East Riding, was not primarily a sheep-farming area; its flat fields were ideal for mixed, primarily arable farming, but sheep provided an important seasonal income, as did pigs and cattle for beef and milk production. As a result, there were hay meadows, longstanding grazing land, and larger fields that were never brought into the system of crop rotation, as well as the paddocks and orchards close to the farmyards. These undisturbed acres were rich in wild flowers. Gradually, during the 1930s, tractors began to appear. Their strange panting could be heard as they approached and a new smell invaded the village street; this was the future of farming, but we could not then have imagined the enormous fields of the post-Second World War era, cultivated by one lone man.

The activities of the farming year provided the framework to village life. Three occasions in particular, hay-time, harvest and potato-picking, drew in every member of the family and others who needed part-time work. Fine weather was not predictable; 'Make hay while the sun shines' was the reality. A wet spell could ruin any crop, but rarely did so completely. There were occasions when hay mildewed in the fields, or corn was laid flat by thundery rain and couldn't be gathered, or sprouted in the ears before a dry spell came, or when the potatoes got scab and the crop was blighted and poor; but usually something could be salvaged by sheer hard work. As Mrs Charlie Robinson would say in a late or wet season, 'They've allus getten t'arvest in, an' they allus will.' When the weather was kind, everyone took a share in the work: there were baskets of 'drinkings' to be taken down to the fields, hay to be tossed and turned, bound sheaves to be piled into tent-shaped stooks to ripen and dry, and a chance to ride home on the last cart at the end of the day. Harvest Festival, in September, was indeed a time of thanksgiving and celebration for a harvest safely gathered in. The school had a fortnight's holiday for potato-picking in October, and women and children were in the fields on hands and knees with baskets, 'taty scrattin' – clawing the potatoes out of the ground as they were turned up, trying to ensure that every last one was gathered, to avoid unwanted plants emerging among the following year's different crop.

This was the working village I knew by observation only, the background to my life, seen from the house and garden and when walking in the lanes. So what was my own experience of the neighbourhood in which others worked and made a living? My mother and I walked, and every walk was an adventure: there were such treasures to be found, such experiences. One regular walk was along Boat Lane, the road to Aldwark Bridge, alongside Kirby Hall Park. As we turned into it, the drive to the house was on the right hand side, with the lodge by its gate, a relic from grander days. It stood empty for a long time while I was very young, but, after Mrs Thirkill's husband was killed when a tractor overturned and she was deprived of the tied cottage that went with his job, she was allowed to rent it and live there with her children.

Just past the lodge was the ice house, shaped like the Eskimo's igloo in our geography picture. It was set on a rise and made of brick, which even then was beginning to crumble. There was nothing to be seen if you peered through the grating at the entrance because the storage area had been filled in; but, when it functioned as a store in Lord Knaresborough's day, it had a deep, brick-lined pit, sunk well into the earth, to hold meat and game packed in ice, which was available commercially even then. In those cold conditions it didn't melt quickly and preserved the contents for as long as required. The surrounding mound was tunnelled with rabbit holes and I've since wondered if it had been a managed rabbit warren. We used to clap our hands as we went

113

past and watch the white scuts of the rabbits bobbing away, and down to safety.

Across the road from the ice house was the violet gate. This was just an ordinary field entrance with a rough, worn gate, but on each side of it was a large patch of violets, deep purple and heavily scented in the flowering season, and at intervals along the hedgerow were a few white ones. When they were at the peak of perfection, I would pick a bunch and arrange them in moss in a shallow, ruby-glass bowl of water to put in the living room. The memory of going up to the bowl and breathing in deeply that bitter-sweet mingled smell of sweet violets and earthy moss is with me still.

The verge along Boat Lane, like all the verges on the hard-topped roads and green lanes, was cut at intervals with drainage channels, very effective in keeping the roads and cart tracks free of water, and enabling it to seep into the ditches that lay on the road side of every hedge. This road and its verges were immaculately maintained by Percy Cuthbert. The channels gave our walks an added interest in frosty weather when they had a skimming of ice. If there was water under the ice, it was dark and solid and you could slide on it; if there was hardly any water, the ice was light in colour, creaked if you stood on it, and could be hammered into fragments with a shoe heel or by jumping.

Sometimes we went the whole way down Boat Lane, past the bluebell wood on the right, past the riverside farms, to the toll gate at Aldwark Bridge. The Coupland family lived in the tiny toll house on the left hand side of the road, perched above a sloping track leading down to the river. Their job was to take the fee for crossing the bridge into the North Riding and open the gate. For foot passengers it cost one halfpenny each way, for bicycles one penny, and more for horses and carts and motor vehicles. Mrs Coupland, like most village women, was always ready to chat, and this was another house where we occasionally had tea and cake. When we had paid our toll, she opened the pedestrian gate and we went through. I fussed about crossing the bridge; it frightened me. The track was made entirely of wood, bolted to the metal structure, with substantial planks laid lengthways to smooth the path of vehicles, and others laid at right angles to them. The bridge had taken a lot of hard wear, and there were gaps between the eroded edges of the short planks, where you could see the river flowing swiftly underneath. I was convinced that it would give way and drop me into the water; I had no faith in the structure that held it all together. I couldn't be persuaded to look through the struts of the bridge into the water for more than a moment, but would stand safely at the far side and watch the flow of the river from the security of firm land. There might be a boat making its way downstream to York, someone fishing, or sand martins popping in and out of their nests on the far bank. Then we would walk a little way towards Aldwark before making the hazardous return crossing. If we had to wait for a horse and cart to cross, there would be clip-clopping, rumbling and clanking as it crossed the planks safely one by one, but I was still convinced that there was a plank just waiting to collapse under my weight.

Our second and more usual option was to turn left from Boat Lane onto Cross Lane, the roughly rutted green lane giving access to the fields behind Great Ouseburn and leading into Church Lane, from which you could return to the village. Its wide verges were full of wild flowers, scrubby patches of burnet roses, knapweed, cow parsley tough grass. The hedges in Church Lane were tall, with early blackthorn, the best place to see the first hazel catkins and look for the little red female flowers; later, may blossom, wild roses and honeysuckle scented the air and, with the budding blackberry bushes and hedge maple, promised autumn glory and a profusion of fruit. There were horse chestnuts alongside the dank, sunken area by Miss Thompson's field, and the field opposite had not yet been set aside for the cemetery and was grazed by horses. The main lane curved round, past the back gate of the churchyard, and round again to the Barn Hall and out into the village street, but there was a branch off to the left leading to the back of Burrell's yard and the Oddfellows' allotments. If you went ahead and didn't turn towards the allotments, a narrow, dark path, Tommy Lane, lay between the high churchyard wall and an equally high one flanking Kirkholme. Footsteps and voices echoed and it smelt of damp, crumbly rendered stone, algae and wet moss, but it was a well used short cut to the village street.

Turning away from the village as you entered Church Lane from Cross Lane, you could go further along in the direction of the river and look into a small, wet area of verge, almost a pond, where, in spring, there was always frog spawn. Eventually the lane became a gated track into farm land through which you reached the river.

In summer, when the fields were dry, we often took a short cut from Cross Lane into a pasture rich with quaking grass and wild flowers in season, from cowslips through to ox-eye daisies, betony, salad burnet, sorrels, knapweed, pignut, and varieties of clover, all lost to the wartime mandate to plough up this priceless heritage. We then went through the headland of the cornfield, with knot grass, scarlet pimpernel, tiny speedwells and forget-me-nots, eyebright, spurrey, poppies, corn marigolds, the occasional corn cockle, and from there through the cricket field and back home. These walks never lost their charm; as a teenager burdened with examination revision, I would walk the longer circuit on summer evenings, alone in the friendly landscape, reciting poetry or history notes to the empty fields and familiar trees.

A longer walk would take us along Carr Side, to Little Ouseburn via the high road, through the village, past Moat Hall and the church, over the bridge and back home. At the corner where Carr Side joins the high road was the workhouse. On sunny afternoons the old people would be sitting out in the doorway, facing the sun. We always stopped to look at the sign in the garden marking Ouse Gill spring, the spot where the Ouse rises out of the ground to form my well-loved little stream, the beck running behind the village and through Kirby Hall Park. When parish charity was replaced by state welfare the building stood empty. During the war it housed prisoners of war, who worked on the land. Redundant again, it became Campbell and Penty's seed warehouse, marred by white dust, looking shamefully neglected, with shabby, overgrown gardens.

This was home ground. In my early teens my mother and I cycled further afield, across the river, past the aerodrome to the village of Linton-on-Ouse, or to Alne and Easingwold; through Upper Dunsforth to Low Dunsforth and on to Aldborough and Boroughbridge; to Whixley and Cattal, past the anti-aircraft station and small air base, perhaps turning instead to Cowthorpe to look again at the Cowthorpe Oak, the most ancient tree in the locality; occasionally we even went through Marton-cum-Grafton and across the Great North Road to Knaresborough.

The walks, the lanes, all had their charm: simple, familiar pleasures, they matched the expectations of a country child. My mother was virtually my sole companion, except when the uncles or Ken came to visit; but, when I could roam in Jackson's field or walk alone, I escaped into the delights of solitude; I loved to be in the open air, looking at what was around, welcoming the seasons, delighting in the rediscovery of old friends, such as the first celandine, or the familiar companions, bluebell and greater stitchwort, or yellow rattle, or the sequential vetches, yellow, pink and purple, scrambling in the hedgerows and verges, and the bright bryony and white convolvulus. Here, caressed by the gentle breeze or warmed by the sun, or delighted by the song of birds and their busy fluttering in the hedgerows and free flight overhead, or cooled by the scented evening air, or just listening to the silence enhanced by a distant sound, I found healing for passing fears and distresses; I was content.

CHAPTER IX

In the mind's eye

It is May, six o'clock in the morning on the magic first of May. I know the rhyme and now it's time for an act of faith. It's there in my book of poems for children:

> The fair maid who on the first of May
> Goes to the fields at break of day,
> And washes in dew from the hawthorn tree
> Will ever after handsome be.

It isn't exactly dawn, but my dad isn't up yet, so it's as near as I can hope for. Anticipation trembling in my stomach, I dress quietly, creep downstairs. The tall tree in the corner of the girls' yard won't do, but the one in Jacksons' field near the gate fits the description and I can reach the soft young leaves. The grass is cool and wet to my sandalled feet and, yes, the leaves are bright with dew. I soak my hands and rub them over my face, enjoying the tingling coldness of the water on my warm skin. Nobody has seen me; so that's my secret and I slip back into the garden, sit on the swing, and begin my regular exercise on sunny mornings, vigorously swinging and singing at the top of my voice until it's time to go in for breakfast and, on this occasion, try to catch my first May gosling. I don't expect miracles, but perhaps I shall look a little more appealing next time my dad takes a photo of me peering, watery-eyed, into the sun while he adjusts the focus.

Jacksons' field, my delight in all seasons: candles blooming on the horse chestnut tree near the road; spring lambing time, and the sight and sound of new lambs tottering their first steps, skipping about in groups, all four legs off the ground and bodies wriggling, pausing to check on their mothers; the constant interplay of bleats between mothers and babies; tails wagging as they feed. Alongside the marshy bottom of the field, its soft ground pitted with hoof prints, golden with marsh marigolds and dotted with milkmaids and spotted orchis, a firm track leads to a wooden bridge giving the cattle access to the carr land beyond, wet in winter, but allowing extra grazing in summer, smelling of herby mud, stale water and cow dung dotted with smooth, spiky-tipped rushes, triangular-stemmed sedges, ragged robin, and meadowsweet to bury your nose in. The bridge is the place from which to float pieces of rush downstream and fish for 'tiddlers' to keep overnight in a jam jar with a bit of water weed and return to the stream the following day. The stream-side smell is familiar and welcoming; water mint, red and white valerian, figwort and brooklime speedwell are friends and companions with names to echo in the mind. The 'island' lies on the left beyond the wooden bridge. Even in the driest months you have to brave a patch of wet, sticky mud to get onto it, and the plants and reeds, taller than a child, grow in soggy ground along the stream where it opens into shallow water. I never venture there alone.

As spring passes into summer, the grass grows longer in the field, rested briefly from grazing. What utter joy to run and tumble in it, turning five or six somersaults in succession, and then spin round until the world turns! Soon the cows graze and crop it short, spreading brown cow-claps across the green, attracting horse flies and bluebottles. Their paths are trodden again and there's a heart-thumping adventure for the daring. Down in the damp part of the field, nearer the pond, is a narrow, marshy gully, with an unpredictable depth of water and a squelchy, soft bottom. This is welly country; perhaps this time the water will come over the tops; better not to walk right along it, just in case I sink! Next, run across the grass and through the meadowsweet to the wide stretch of water edged with coarse-leaved reeds and greater willowherb. The cows have trodden their muddy drinking hole, liberally laced with treacherously tacky offerings, but ideal for skimming pebbles; four or five bounces if you choose the flat ones and get the angle right. Persistent smell of decaying leaves and water mint, just like the tiddler stream. It's time to make a new fishing net, and beg a jar and a piece of string to tie round the neck for a handle. The uncles have come to stay: we can play cricket in the flat part of the field near the house and Uncle Harry will come and skim pebbles; he first showed me how to do it properly and he's good at it. Autumn and acorns; always the hunt to find the biggest one. They are brown and shiny as they shed their perfect little cups with the stalks at an angle; pity you can't eat them. The wind brings down twigs; I collect every scrap in a basket for firewood; satisfied, I carry it home.

Winter and snow; take the short cut and squeeze through the gap made by twisting the fourth and fifth metal railings in the corner of the yard and run through the snow; scoop and throw it; admire the pattern of longer grasses above the unspoilt, gleaming whiteness. Hard, persistent frost, and the shallow pond is frozen. People bring skates and we younger ones slide. I fall hard on my bottom and hurt my tail-bone, but I don't confess because I'd not be allowed to go again. Such a freeze-up doesn't happen often and it won't last long. But never mind; the blackbirds will soon be singing and again it will be spring. Yes, Jacksons' field, a friend for all seasons.

Birds: fussy, loose-bibbed sparrows and their mates busy in the playground when the boys have gone, looking for crumbs from packed lunches, perching on roofs, chirping and squabbling in trees and bushes; the stone in the rockery where the thrush hammers snails; the perky robin, determined not to miss a grub when the soil is turned; the first April cuckoo, its song loud on still days in May; the swallows' busy season; gulls following the plough; crows and rooks loud and low, crossing the empty fields; flocks of starlings raiding the stubble; a heron standing on the edge of the pond, perfectly reflected, patiently fishing. Evening, and as the birds roost, the bats come out of the belfry and wheel round the school buildings, dark against the sky. Just before I go to sleep, the owls hoot.

It's a gloomy, stifling day, with gathering thunder clouds. As always in such weather, the rumble of the train approaching Cattal station and its shrill whistle seem loud and close on the still air. A bell tolls from little Ouseburn church, a single, deep pealing, slowly repeated. It's Jackie Wighton's funeral; Jackie, the eldest boy of the family, not much older than me, gentle and cheerful, died of a brain tumour. His death leaves me bewildered; death is not just something that happens to older people; the bell threatens chill mortality.

We're back from Scarborough. As usual, we left immediately after an early breakfast and now it's late morning. The seaside smells of sand, seaweed and salt air, the thriving working harbour with a load of timber, the Dutch herring fleet, the sailors' clogs clattering on the piers and pavements, the fish market just across the road from our boarding house, Scott's fish and chip shop where we sat for fish suppers or carried out hot, fresh chips in newspaper; all these, so welcome in anticipation, so enjoyable in their context, give way to country sights and sounds and smells; the ripened harvest, binders in the fields and carts carrying loads of stooks, shedding wisps along the road; keen fresh air scented with vegetation and damp soil; the garden a riot of plants grown beyond belief in the two, even three weeks of August when we've been on holiday. It's a benison just to run out and stand amongst it, breathing it all in; it's good to be home.

Fishing: my dad loves fishing. Every season he buys a fishing permit and gets permission from several local farmers to use the stretch of river on which they own the right to fish. Public fishing is permitted on both sides of Aldwark Bridge, if you have a licence. In summer time we often take a picnic down there on a fine day. I play in the dry sand of the left hand bank, hold one of the rods for a while and watch the float, help to bait the hooks with a worm or a couple of fat, white, writhing maggots fresh from the stinking sawdust and rotting meat in which my dad has bred them. Or my mother and I take a walk along the bank to the right of the bridge and watch water voles popping in and out of the vegetation and scrounging around the muddy grasses where the steep bank joins the water, before slipping smoothly into the river and paddling along to a new patch. On this occasion I'm four or five. Ken is staying with us and I've pushed my doll's pram with Ted in it all the way to the bridge – with a bit of help, perhaps. Thunder threatens and big drops of rain begin to fall. We hastily pack up. My dad pushes his bike with the fishing basket and tackle, my mother carries the picnic bag. Ken lifts me into the doll's pram, a miniature version of my own, and runs with me all the way home. We're home first, but we all get very wet.

Winter frosts; thick icicles hanging from the gutters, fern patterns on every window, the kitchen pump refusing to deliver water; then dark, cold, rainy days with biting winds. Winter brings the epidemics. Last year it was scarlet fever and measles; this year it's diphtheria and whooping cough. Several people in the village are in the isolation hospital. Leslie Mothersdale is said to be very ill. With the outbreak of a serious notifiable disease the school is closed for fumigation by a local authority team. When it is pronounced safe, Mr and Mrs Smith give everything a thorough cleaning before it reopens. I've only had a cold, but Ivy has been away from school for several weeks with whooping cough. I miss her very much. When she comes back I'm intrigued by her loud, indrawn gasping breath as she coughs, the symptom which lingers for a long time, particularly after a bad attack.

The caretaker's wash kitchen is a warm, bright lure on winter Saturday mornings and pulsates with heat in summer. It's in the same range of buildings as ours, with its own chimney, but separated from them by our back-yard wall. I'm not allowed to go in there, but I hang around the open door. The fire is burning brightly and the set pot is full of hot water, the steam rising round the edges of the wooden cover. There are cans of sawdust, long-handled sweeping brushes with hard or soft bristles, hand brushes, dust pans, scrubbing brushes, yellow bar soap, a kneeling mat, zinc buckets and a mopping bucket with a strainer to squeeze out water from the soggy rag mop. The air smells of ashy heat and soft soap from the big open can, from which Mrs Smith scoops a dollop to put in the water for mopping the stone floors of the cloakrooms between scrubbings; there's a smell of Jeyes' Fluid, used to disinfect the toilet cans and urinal walls, and underlying it the sickly smell lingering in the brushes kept for the oil used on the wooden classroom floors during the long holidays. It's stored in a large, yellow-stained drum with sticky dribbles down its sides. Oil is the smell of the new school year.

For routine sweeping Mrs Smith uses a scattering of sawdust to clean the surface where the day's dirt has stuck to the oiled boards. Coarse wood they may be, but they are well preserved.

Spring cleaning, and Mrs Smith comes to help. She washes the furniture with vinegar and water and polishes it with Mansion Polish. There is always an accumulation of ingrained dust and ash from the fireplaces, so she and my father fold the heavy carpets and carry them out into Jacksons' field to clean them and brighten the colours by trailing them across the grass. Lino is scrubbed; rag rugs are given an extra beating on the clothes line and trailed across the grass in their turn. Everything is excitingly out of place, exposing the patches of normally unreachable dirt under the heavy furniture; curtains are taken down for shaking or washing; the sofa and armchairs have been carried into the yard and beaten; they invite bouncing. Two full days see the job completed, but it was good while it lasted.

Dread invades the school day, a counterpoint to lessons; the cod liver oil room has been taken over by the school dentist, appropriately named Mr Buzza. He's a handsome, freckled, reassuring man with a mass of wavy chestnut hair and a Scots accent, and he's going to darken my days once a year until I'm seventeen. Even at Knaresborough Grammar School he was the spectre stalking the corridors from his den in the senior mistress's room. My first experiences of Mr Buzza's ministrations, though, were cod-liver-oil-scented. He set up his chair and foot-operated drill and inspected our open mouths with a metal mirror, carefully probing every tooth and its setting in the gum with a sharp instrument, looking increasingly serious, and finally delivering his verdict. Occasionally there would be good news – nothing more to be done; more often than not a milk tooth must be prematurely extracted, or a filling would be needed. The syringe for injections was thick and painful; the foot-operated drill bumbled and ground over the tooth, wobbling its way noisily into the decaying patch. He exchanged pleasantries with my father on the way out at the end of the day and gave me a warm smile as he passed through the playground, but his mere presence in the school could blight my days as I waited for the nurse to call my name.

The feeling of release when they've all gone, visitors, teachers and caretakers! The playground and the school are all mine and I don't have to relate to anyone else. I can ponder over the beauty and softness of the hawthorn petals on the tree in the corner, take in their scent. I can warm to the glowing, ripe berries in season and smell the bitter, autumn smell of darkening leaves. I can speed my scooter from one end of the girls' playground to the other; I can ride my bike round and round both yards; I can play ball against the wall, honing my skills, or hit a tennis ball against the rough stone kitchen wall with a racquet, skilfully responding to its erratic bouncing, and pretend that I am playing at Wimbledon. I can play my own game of marbles in the holes we all use and warm my legs in the late afternoon sun on the iron plates that cover the chutes to the stoke hole, and smell the nearby roses. I can take the keys and go into the infants' classroom to squat by the library box, knowing that nobody will interrupt me. I can go into the greenhouse to see what's growing; perhaps dip the rabbit's tail into the flowers of sulphur and put a bit onto the tomato plants or chrysanthemum cuttings. I can wander round the whole garden, swing, pick something to eat, poke caterpillars off the cabbages and see them curl round the stick, watch the young cockerels squaring up to each other and laugh at their first attempts to crow, collect eggs and speak to Peepy. I can sit on a concrete slab by the pond my dad made in the little garden on the other side of the garage from the swing and enjoy the smooth, slow movement of the goldfish, give them some excitement by putting a pinch of ants' eggs into the water, admire the ash tree in the corner that he planted the year I was born; it's quite tall now. When the blue tits have hatched, I listen at the wall between the playgrounds and hear them whistling in their nest in the crevice; I know the crack underneath the big window of my dad's classroom where there's a new brood every year. I like to be alone, to look at things and enjoy them as they are, listen to the sounds around me, listen to my inner voice and hold a conversation with myself, away from my parents and other children, free just to be me.

The years have sped by; the long day of double summer time is drawing to a close. Distant droning; gradually the air fills with sound. Here they come, the squadrons, gathering from the north, dark shapes, deadly mechanical birds, beautiful with the beauty of the machine, outlined against the serene, golden sky. Revving crescendos to the east, and the Lancasters of Linton-on-Ouse rise to join them; by the direction of flight probably the Ruhr again or maybe Berlin. 'Good luck, boys. That's for London and Coventry and York.' Warm darkness creeps down on the blacked-out houses and they blend into the fields and trees. I go indoors. Though I don't know it, the door has already closed on the past: the village of my childhood, like childhood itself, is a memory.

PART II

GROWING UP IN WARTIME

Interlude

I have thought of this recollection as 'a quiet war'. A small village in the Vale of York was a backwater compared with cities and towns devastated by air raids, or areas that witnessed the Battle of Britain, the retreat from Dunkirk, the D Day offensive, the steady return of casualties to the Channel ports. The part played in the war by our locality was among the most significant in the government's overall strategy, but its impact on people living there was less intrusive and more continuous than the experiences of those more directly targeted by the enemy; our rural way of life went on largely undisturbed, dictated more by the demands of everyday life and the seasons than by the fact that the nation was at war.

We were situated along the chain of airfields in the East of England used by Group 4, Bomber Command, with its headquarters at Heslington Hall, York. They had been established in the mid-1930s in anticipation of a war with Hitler's Reich and were developed and extended once hostilities began in order to carry out a sustained bombing campaign against targets in Germany and the occupied territories. Air raid warnings were comparatively frequent because of our position between two of these airfields, Dishforth and Linton-on-Ouse, and very close to several more small airfields used during the war as the force expanded. We were constantly aware of aerial activity: pre-operational practice and the activity of smaller aircraft by day, redeployment of squadrons which moved frequently between bases; the upgrading of aircraft, pulses of intense action during the evenings as the bombers set off on their nightly missions, the sporadic attempts by German aircraft to destroy the airfields, the searchlight beams and intense barrages from anti-aircraft batteries dotted around the neighbourhood. During the night we were sometimes aware of the sound of returning aircraft, but usually we ignored them and slept.

Nevertheless, we always knew that, at any moment, day or night, everything could change. When the air-raid warden, ringing a hand-bell, went through the village there was the quickened heartbeat, the thought that life could end here and now, the feeling that the safest place was the damp space under the stairs, lit only by a paraffin lamp, no longer my father's darkroom for the alchemy by which he had developed and printed photographs. Eventually, we learned to live with the experience and didn't bother to take shelter, being fairly sure that the village was not a target.

When asked by my young grandson what it had been like to live in wartime, I felt that I had very little to tell, because my family spent the war years in a village virtually untouched by catastrophic events; but our experience was probably that of many British people outside the areas most affected by enemy action. Such an unsensational story has not often been written, focusing, as it must, on life below the much-recorded drama of the skies which was converted to simple statistics in the media as it unfolded. It is hard to identify what was distinctively the wartime experience and what was routine daily life as I would have known it regardless of the war. Though there were some changes, I went to school, progressed through the classes, made friendships, learned new skills, walked and cycled round the locality, lived my home life much as I would have done in peace or war. What I aim to do, then, is to give the flavour of growing up in wartime, the daily focal point of my teenage years being the BBC evening news bulletins telling of fighting on land, at sea and in the air, of military engagements in distant places which, if not brought to a successful conclusion, could destroy our familiar British way of life. Sometimes these events came closer to home, particularly after Dunkirk with the fear of invasion, knowing that other European nations, including France, were under Nazi occupation; that disasters were occurring to other people elsewhere in England as the bombs fell, always knowing, but with a sense of unreality, that my own life was vulnerable.

In a much more personal sense, though, I was reluctant to re-experience this part of my life, because something fundamental had changed. By the time war was declared I was no longer a young child; the magic and immediacy and timelessness of those early years had gone and I was tied to the rigorous demands of an academic education. The practicalities of completing all that needed to be done here and now, tonight and tomorrow, left little room for the observer, the person with freedom to savour the small things, the world of the senses, the life of the imagination. It was there still, around the edges, that timeless world where living moment by moment had the freshness of a new adventure and leisure to open the mind to the here and now, but I was different. I was about to embark on the uncharted sea of the teens, with its anxieties and insecurities, its need to achieve and a different kind of self-consciousness.

When I first started writing this second part of my experiences of life in the Vale of York I intended that the various phases of the war would be markers to the passing of time, the main narrative being how wartime changes in our family life influenced my development from childhood to adulthood and shaped some of my abiding values. Indeed, I have not referred directly to many of the campaigns that made this catastrophe into a world war; such events merely formed a background to my personal life as they were reported in the news. In this narrowly focused picture the proximity of the local RAF bases was to be included as the distinguishing feature of our area. What I did not envisage was the impact of what I learned about the role of Bomber Command on my understanding of my own neighbourhood. Gradually I began to see in human terms the significance of what I was reading and came to understand more fully what I had witnessed and interpreted simplistically as a young observer and rarely reconsidered once the war was over and I moved on into professional and family life. As a result, the personal story has been illuminated by retrospective historical insights, though it remains primarily what it set out to be, an account of what it was like to be a village child growing up and leaving home in wartime. The more I think about this period of my life the more I recognize the significance of that grim juxtaposition of the horrific and the mundane and the helplessness of the general population in times of war and of the young men and women caught up in fighting, conscripted to serve their country whatever that may demand of them. For us at home in a Yorkshire village, life went on, ordinary daily life; for many others, it didn't.

It was easy in wartime, influenced by government propaganda, to call up facile responses to the notion of a fight for our democratic way of life against an enemy who would destroy the values we stood for as a nation. It was possible to depersonalize not only the enemy, but those 'heroes' who were fighting our battle for us on every front. It is always possible to argue a convincing case in the abstract, and in any national emergency the official propaganda machine swings into action, massaging unpalatable truths, shaping opinion, avoiding presenting any perception which might undermine the morale of people in all walks of life who are being asked to make sacrifices and may undergo unspeakable suffering. Officially, and in the constructed mind of the public, there is simple duty: if you're not prepared to support your country, you're a traitor; if you're a conscientious objector you may well be a coward, always that shadow of doubt. More than sixty years after the events described here, I am left with an overwhelming sense of sadness at the sheer destructive waste of it all and a deep-rooted fear that human beings will never co-operate internationally and build the better world we thought we were fighting for. Too many vested interests and too much national pride and prejudice stand in the way.

Does that mean that I'm a total pessimist? Not at all. We live our lives as individuals, trying to be the best we can and do whatever we can to create around us out of our own experience the love and harmony that make life so richly worth living. We willingly make our small sacrifices to promote and serve the causes that stir our loyalties; we make our mistakes and sometimes fail, but we use our opportunities to build the unique structure which is one person's lifetime, and leave its memory behind with those who have known us. This second part of my account of life in the quiet vale and beyond is not now what at first I thought it would be, because it is informed by retrospect. Hopefully, as a result of the intense experience of looking beyond the personal dimension, I have made it richer and more thought-provoking.

CHAPTER X

From peace to war

The years 1938 and 1939 were an uneasy period in British history. Tantalized by the hope of peace, fearful of the prospect of war, those who had seen it all before were apprehensive about the future. As a twelve year old I was only vaguely aware of international events. When my uncles Ernest and Harry, my mother's brothers, came on their regular visits there would be gloomy talk of the inevitability of another war. My uncle Harry had been wounded in the leg and spent over two years as a prisoner of war in Germany; my father had been a stretcher bearer with the King's Own Yorkshire Light Infantry; my mother, as a college student, had experienced the privations of wartime, the anxiety of knowing that her fiancé was serving on the battlefield and the sadness of her brother's being reported as 'wounded and missing' before news of his imprisonment came through.

The background to this resurgent anxiety, of which I was only vaguely aware, was the regular reporting of Hitler's increasing aggression in Europe. German forces marched into Austria on 12 March, 1938[2] and declared it a province of the Third Reich. The Czechs began mobilization, reluctantly backed by France and Britain. In September trouble flared in Sudetenland, where most of the country's German-speaking

---

[2] Edward Davidson and Dale Manning, *Chronology of World War Two* (London: Cassell, 1999), 11. This book has provided precise details about general campaigns and has been used throughout for factual information without frequent attribution.

inhabitants were living: encouraged by Hitler, they had been pressing for union with Germany and were urged by him to direct action on 12 September. The Czech government quelled the rebellion and Neville Chamberlain flew to Munich with a plan, not previously discussed with France, that those parts of Czechoslovakia whose people voted for it should be ceded to Germany. France agreed reluctantly, but Hitler wanted more concessions and Chamberlain, prepared to be accommodating, was outvoted in parliament. By 23 September the Czechs were fully mobilized and the British and French, represented by Chamberlain and Daladier, returned to Munich for further talks. Before returning, Chamberlain persuaded Hitler to sign a 'friendship' document and came back from Munich to reassure the nation that this represented 'peace in our time'.

There was a sense of temporary reprieve, but no optimism. The spring of 1939 saw Britain and France sending guarantees of support to Poland, Greece and Roumania and the introduction of conscription in Britain in May. On 31 August, 1939, in spite of last-minute attempts at diplomacy, Hitler gave orders for the invasion of Poland, which began the following day. Chamberlain's appeasement policy had clearly failed, though it had provided a valuable opportunity for Britain to push forward with rearmament; so the British cabinet sent an ultimatum to Hitler on 2 September to the effect that these hostilities must cease by 11 am on 3 September, or the two countries would be at war.

For me, largely unaware of these developments and their significance, the summer of 1939 marked a change in the established pattern of family life. I had met Doris Davies, my cousin Ken's fiancée and looked forward to their wedding, in spite of my unwillingness to share my long-time companion during school holidays, the kindly tease, the serious listener and confiding friend. I might even be bridesmaid. No such luck. As I have always understood it, Doris became probably the only girl ever to become engaged with a sewing machine instead of a ring and, shortly before term ended, they were married during the lunch hour in the registry office in Barking, where they taught at the same school, and went back to school in the afternoon.

When the Germans invaded Poland on 1 September, the government imposed a blackout on London and began the evacuation of over a million school children in anticipation of the forthcoming declaration of war. Ken and Doris were involved in this and accompanied their school. I don't know where they went, or for how long they remained involved, but very soon Ken left teaching for a reserved occupation as an aircraft inspector in the Ministry of Aircraft Production based at Trafford Park in Manchester and they moved into a rented Edwardian terrace house in Monton, near Eccles, a few hundred yards from Ken's father's post office, taking Doris's mother with them. In post-war London, where property had been severely damaged by the blitz, Ken could not find a house for them to live in which would have enabled him to take up his reserved teaching post in Barking; so they remained in Monton, taught in the local area, brought up their family there, eventually bought the house and stayed in it for the rest of their lives.

The second change was the wedding in August, 1939, of my cousin Madge, daughter of my father's brother, Uncle John, to Lewis Davies, brother of her college friend, Eileen. Once again I hoped to be bridesmaid, but she asked Eileen and another friend. I consoled myself with the thought that everyone would have stared at me and I wouldn't have known what to do, as we'd never gone to church as a family. All I remember about the wedding is that my mother made me a dress with a blue skirt and a mustard-coloured top, with a matching blue bolero jacket to go over it. I wore a hat, home made from the same fabric as the top of the dress, and my first pair of high-heeled shoes (well, not flat!). To my mother's annoyance, Madge asked if she could borrow her wedding veil and managed to tear it. We had food somewhere and photographs were taken outside their family house in Leeds. I felt very uncomfortable, the only child among so many strangers. Madge and Lew had bought a semi-detached house in Camberley near his work at the Royal Aircraft Establishment at Farnborough, where he, too, was in a reserved occupation.

Shortly after the wedding we went on holiday to Scarborough and stayed with Mr and Mrs Boyes in our usual boarding house in the South Bay opposite the fish pier. It was always a delight to go back to Scarborough. My dad hated driving and insisted on getting up at four o'clock in the morning, an adventure in itself, to be through the Malton bottle-neck before the hold-ups, which were notorious even in the 1930s. We arrived for breakfast at about eight o'clock, ready to settle into our familiar holiday routine. This involved walking in the gardens or along the harbour front or on the piers, eating fish and chips from Scott's and ice creams from Pacitto's, spending a few pennies at the fun-fairs, watching my father fishing from the pier or sharing his delight when the man who had failed to guess his weight correctly returned his money. When it was warm enough I would paddle, even be allowed to wear my bathing costume and get wet. Whenever possible, while my parents sat in deck chairs, I would play on the sands, making sand castles or a boat in sand with a seat to sit on. My mother would take me along to have an occasional donkey ride, or the three of us would watch a Punch and Judy show; always in my heart of hearts I longed for young company and wished I could join other children playing ball games nearby.

In the afternoons, while my father rested and read cowboy or mystery stories borrowed for twopence a week from Boots' holiday lending library, my mother and I went on the dodgem cars, or I rode a horse on a roundabout or, my favourite occupation, we explored the rock pools at low tide, enjoying the metallic smell of the sand and seaweed. We carefully selected pebbles and shells looked at sea urchins, starfish, tiny crabs and shrimps, and drank and filled Tusie's portable cup from the iron-rich water trickling from its source in the spa. Sometimes we went by bus round the Marine Drive to the North Bay, then took the miniature railway to Scalby Mills where there was a booth with a man who had performing fleas, or took a small paddle-boat on the lake in Peasholme Park, and walked or rode back after an ice cream soda in the Corner Cafe by the open-air bathing pool. Tusie accompanied us everywhere, trotting ahead on her lead, or panting in someone's arms. After our evening meal I was allowed to take her for her last walk of the day down Quay Street and back along Sandside.

Every morning my dad and I went out at six-thirty to Whiteleys, a little cafe on the sea-front where we drank Camp coffee, mine made of milk, and ate morning coffee biscuits before going to watch the trading at the fish market; this gave my mother a chance to lie in bed a little longer. Fishermen touted for business along the piers, and occasionally we would go out with one of them in his small boat and fish over the side with rod and line. I once caught a flat fish which Mrs Boyes gladly cooked for my breakfast, to my delight. Another regular part of the holiday ritual was to send boxes of kippers, bought from one of the stalls along the quayside, to Mr and Mrs Smith and Mrs Metcalfe.

I welcomed the different smells: of sea air, sand and seaweed, the fish pier itself, fish and chips, even the warm, pungent smell of beer and tobacco from the open pub door near the fish and chip shop. The bustle of a holiday resort and fishing port with a working harbour was exciting: the noise of humanity, the clatter of the clogs of sailors from the Dutch herring fleet which always came into port during our stay, the sirens of the working boats and pleasure steamers entering or leaving the harbour, the unloading of a cargo of Scandinavian wood, the tunny (tuna) fishermen with their latest exhibit, huge fish caught with a rod and line by these wealthy connoisseurs of streamlined boats and expensive tackle. I was happy to fall asleep at night to the sound of revelry in the streets and from the fun fair near the Marine Drive, the lights, the flashing of the lighthouse. It was equally welcome, though, at the end of a fortnight, or even three weeks away, to return to Great Ouseburn, after a very early breakfast, enjoying the fields of ripe corn and sights and sounds of harvest, at the stately thirty miles an hour the Jowett and my father found comfortable. I didn't think, in those last few weeks of peace-time, that it would be eight years before I went back to Scarborough to spend a last uneasy holiday with my parents in different accommodation near the North Bay, because the jewellery shop and the large apartment above it where the Boyes family lived, at 1a Sandside, had become the Harbour Bar, or that, by then, I should be a graduate and have met my future husband.

So, in 1939, we returned to the village on a sunny day at the end of August. I rushed out into the garden to breathe in the smells of home – of country air, keen in the nostrils, still moist from the early morning even as the sun gained power, full of the scent of roses and rampant greenery, with the hens prating softly in the background, the tang of poultry; utter joy to relax again into stillness and the comfort of listening to the silence flooding the distance, all the more tangible because of the occasional lowing of cattle, snatches of bird song, a train whistling into Cattal station, the sound of distant machinery in a harvest field; back, also, to a new reality which would reshape our lives, as the international situation hastened towards crisis.

September came and we listened anxiously to the news to hear how Hitler had responded to the British ultimatum, fearful rather than hopeful. The Prime Minister, Neville Chamberlain, was to address the nation on the radio at 11.15 on 3 September. Even as a twelve-year-old looking forward to my 13th birthday I sensed the solemnity of these events, and shared my parents' apprehension. I felt that some personal response should mark the occasion and my own incredulity that this could really be happening. I went into the rock garden, where the sun was hot on my face and warming the path under my feet; I stared down the field towards the fish-pond bridge and Little Ouseburn church, all so serene, secure and familiar, slightly hazy in the heat. I touched the petals of a particularly beautiful flower and said aloud, 'England is at peace.' Then I went into the house to listen to Chamberlain's announcement that Germany had ignored the ultimatum. 'A state of war now exists between Great Britain and Germany.' I returned to the flower, touched it again and said, 'England is at war.' This little ceremony underlined the gravity of the occasion. It seemed very unreal, but I was afraid, deeply afraid, because of its utterly unknowable consequences, and my imagination was filled with melodramatic horrors.

When my mother and I had cycled on pleasant afternoons to Linton-on-Ouse, three miles away, eager to see the new aerodrome and watch the planes, we had not known anything about its connection with the hasty plan by the government to fortify the country against the perceived threat from German militarism and redress some of Britain's weakness in air power. Bomber Command had been formed on 17 July 1936 and the two-engined Whitley was the first of the heavy bombers to be deployed at the new airfields. The prototype had flown as recently as 17 March, 1936, and the first planes were stationed at Dishforth in July 1937.[3] They had a good range, in spite of the fact that they could not carry heavy loads, and flew on various missions from local airfields for much of the war.

We had become increasingly aware of the Whitleys. At first they had been a novelty as they flew overhead in training, but in recent months the aerial activity had been constantly increasing. After the declaration of war it was suddenly intensified: these planes from the local aerodromes, including nine from Linton, were used immediately to drop propaganda leaflets over Hamburg, Bremen and the Ruhr, an activity which we heard about in news bulletins without appreciating that local planes had been involved.[4] Such forays continued regularly until late January, 1940, but were abandoned in early April when the RAF began the policy of attacking land targets. The first of these attacks on 19 March, 1940 against the German seaplane base at Hornum on the island of Sylt, included ten Whitleys from Dishforth.[5]

Within a very short time there were other changes in my personal life as the government's evacuation policy came into immediate effect over the whole country. As headmaster, my father was appointed billeting officer for the villages served by his school, and we had evacuees from Potternewton Lane Junior

---

[3] Robert Jackson, *Before the Storm: The Story of Bomber Command 1939-1942* (London: Arthur Baker Ltd, 1972), 46.

[4] Michael P. Wadsworth, *Heroes of Bomber Command: Yorkshire* (Berkshire: Countryside Books 2007), 20. Ten Whitleys from Linton flew to Leconfield to load up with leaflets within a few hours of the outbreak of war.

[5] Max Hastings, *Bomber Command* (London: Michael Joseph, 1979), 50.

Mixed and Infants' School in Leeds. One of their teachers, Miss Webster, was billeted on us. We knew that her Christian name was Lily, but none of us called her by it and she called my parents Mr and Mrs Nicholl; such was the formality of that generation. Her colleague, Miss Luscott, went to the Pentys in Kirby Hall Park. The old 'cod liver oil room' became a classroom once again and everyone crowded in as best they could; the practicalities passed me by as I was at school in Knaresborough.

We now shared our house with a very pleasant, dark-haired woman in her early thirties who, unlike my mother, had a permanent wave, used lipstick and face powder; whose chosen talcum powder was a pervasive Parma Violet and whose supply of clothing was contained in one suitcase. By that time we had a bathroom and I moved from my larger room to occupy the small bedroom created by the conversion. There was always someone to share family meals, and lively conversation instead of our usual mundane communication. In normal circumstances she lodged in Leeds during term time, but her family farmed at Eyam in Derbyshire, and she told us about its reputation for heroism during the Great Plague: when plague struck, the villagers sacrificed their lives by isolating themselves from other neighbouring villages to avoid spreading the infection. She talked about the Derbyshire well dressings, and laughed when we told her that our village post office was 'just over the hill'. As far as she was concerned, compared with her village in the Peak District, there was no hill!

At Knaresborough Grammar School the change was more radical. Our evacuees were from Cockburn High School in Leeds and we shared accommodation by the simple arrangement that each school had the premises for three days in the week: we went to school on Mondays, Wednesdays and Fridays and they went on Tuesdays, Thursdays and Saturdays. We were given substantial amounts of work to do at home on the other days. We thoroughly approved of this arrangement and hoped it would continue, but the expected air attacks on British cities did not come and by Christmas the evacuees from Potternewton Lane and Cockburn had returned to Leeds. The few pupils who wished to remain in Knaresborough could do so and were allowed to retain the brown Cockburn uniform.

Our school uniforms were to be worn almost to destruction, as clothing rationing eventually made replacements difficult, but the requirement to wear uniform remained a firm principle. We wore green tunics with maroon girdles, white cotton blouses and green- and maroon-striped ties, black wool stockings, and long-legged green knickers which also served as P.E. kit along with a white, short-sleeved, Aertex gym shirt. In winter we had dark-green wool jumpers instead of the white blouses; in summer we could wear a printed cotton dress in green and white, and white ankle socks. Our compulsory hats were dark green, with a narrow brim, maroon piping and the school badge, or dark green velour with wide-brims, a maroon and green braid and badge. Coats were of green gabardine and blazers were maroon with green binding and the school badge on the pocket. The boys wore grey trousers, short until they were in the senior school, with white shirts, the regulation school ties and blazers.

We were proud of our uniform because it set us apart as grammar school pupils, a privileged elite – no embarrassment about that. Even when it became difficult to save enough coupons to replace worn-out clothing, the ethos was such that new uniform had priority over leisure wear. There was an extra allowance of coupons, informally known as 'big feet coupons', for some children, the argument being that children who would grow tall quickly had bigger feet at a certain age than those who wouldn't. I failed to qualify. Tunics became shorter as we grew, white blouses strained across the chest and cuffs frayed at the edges and crept up our arms and tunic pleats opened out from the yoke with varying degrees of unseemliness. Wool shrank in the wash, so stockings weren't washed often enough to prevent them from feeling clammy, and green jumpers developed blue patches under the arms, since antiperspirants weren't in general use, especially by children. We accepted darned elbows, sweat stains and the odd spills on unwashable tunics. We sponged them and pressed the pleats regularly. Few people were shabby, and if we smelled less than fresh we didn't notice it.

In the early days of the war there were other changes. We were issued with gas masks in boxes, to be carried at all times, another burden in addition to our over-laden satchels; and also with identity cards, again to accompany us wherever we went. My number was KRMO.13.3, my parents' numbers being 1 and 2. The gas masks were hung on our chairs in whatever classrooms we occupied. We practised how to respond in the case of an air raid alarm. When the alarm bell sounded through the school we abandoned the lesson and went quickly and in silence to sit outside the classroom in the corridor with our backs to the wall, holding our gas masks. We put them on when we were instructed to do so and breathed in the rubbery smell through the heavy disk, felt the air flapping the soft rubber cheeks and farting gently as we breathed out at our neighbours and laughed uproariously at the sight of each other's faces through the visor. We knew it was just a practice because the siren would have sounded in the town for a genuine raid, but it made a welcome interlude. Our headmaster was a scientist with Anglican affiliation, but his priorities were pragmatic: we fourth-form pupils abandoned religious instruction for lessons in first aid; 'scripture' became the most enjoyable lesson of the week as we learned how to put arms in slings, splint broken limbs, put a patient on a stretcher, and apply a tourniquet to staunch arterial bleeding, a pleasant change from sitting at a desk with our attention wandering intermittently in the wilderness with the Israelites.

At the outbreak of war the lights went out all over Britain. It was mandatory not to show a chink of light from buildings. The air raid wardens had the regular task of supervising the effectiveness of the blackout and would knock at the door if a chink of light could be seen. Our village didn't have street lamps; now the only light in the village street came from the brilliant stars and moon. Cloudy winter nights were very dark indeed. Blackout material was supplied in generous quantities by the West Riding, along with splinter net. Our sewing machine worked overtime as my mother made blackout curtains for the whole school and for our house. The heavy, shiny cloth was densely woven and treated with some chemical which had a distinctive smell when the fabric warmed to the touch; it was very difficult to cut, even with sharp scissors. The oatmeal-coloured splinter net was covered with adhesive on one side and had to be cut to fit each window, which was moistened to glue it in place, a fiddly job for the house and oldest school windows, which had small panes. The same applied at Knaresborough where all our classroom windows had splinter net. I was never curious as who put that in place, but it was done, and there were blackout curtains for the few winter activities that took place after school.

Very soon every signpost in the country was removed in case of a German invasion. It wasn't as chaotic and unthinkable as it would be today because there was no culture of long-distance travel by private transport. In wartime Britain there was little opportunity to travel to unknown places; those who needed to do so had maps and in the country as a whole there was a reasonable network of public transport. The railways had many more branch lines than there are now and people relied on trains and local bus services. It is hard to realize how few people had cars for pleasure or convenience before the war and how rarely those who had a private car could travel once rationing began if, like us, they had no claim to priority; it was roughly a hundred miles a month, the equivalent of three or four journeys into York or Harrogate or a couple to Leeds, and became even smaller as petrol supplies were prioritized more strictly. To ensure that the nation accepted the inevitable, the Ministry of Information began to disseminate propaganda posters, such as, 'Is your journey really necessary?' and advocated 'holidays at home'.

Shortly before the outbreak of war my father had bought new Raleigh bicycles for the three of us in anticipation of shortages. Mine was my first adult bike and although, at first, most cycle rides involved my mother and me as they had always done, it came to represent freedom during my teens. As a break from homework on light evenings I would cycle for twenty minutes at full speed around the Dunsforths or occasionally on Saturdays visit school friends who lived in the local villages. Even the main roads were quiet because of petrol rationing. Farmers and business people had a petrol allowance in accordance with their needs, so there were tractors and commercial delivery vans and gravel lorries going to Linton aerodrome, but little other traffic apart from our regular, infrequent bus services.

Those were the practicalities of everyday life, a gradual acclimatization to change. During the first few months, the 'phony war', very little seemed to happen: my fear of personal disaster faded to background apprehension; life changed, but not radically, and no local catastrophe occurred; even national events were remote. I didn't realize the significance of what I was hearing on the radio, though the names of ships became familiar as Germany concentrated on deploying U-boats, the submarines so effectively disrupting the supply of vital food and materials coming into Europe from the Americas. The propaganda war began as early as 26 September, 1939[6], when Germany claimed to have sunk the British aircraft carrier, *Ark Royal*, which was actually in the Atlantic, searching for the *Graf Spee*, which was already wreaking havoc among the convoys bringing vital supplies to Britain and responsible for the loss of over 50,000 tons of shipping.

The full drama of the hunt for the *Graf Spee* was recorded later by historians. On 10 October, for example, flying the French flag, she stopped and boarded the stricken British steamer *Huntsman*, having intercepted her Mayday signal, and captured secret merchant vessel routing documents. Finally, on 13 December, having been damaged in a costly engagement with the cruisers *Exeter, Ajax and Achilles*, she went into the neutral port of Monte Video for repairs. Her captain, Langsdorff, was persuaded by Allied propaganda that he was surrounded by a naval cordon; when the Uruguayan authorities gave him a deadline to leave the port he took the ship to the entrance of Monte Video harbour and scuttled her. This event, along with routine accounts of action against other named enemy vessels, made comforting headline news, masking the reality. As the Foreign Office and Ministry of Information released selected details of naval activity to the BBC and press, accounts of the activities of British ships involved in engagements, and accounts

---

[6] *Chronology*, 17. Activities of *Graf Spee*, selected from 17-22.

of their activities began to form the background to our daily lives.

At the time we didn't realize the critical nature of the loss of merchant shipping, despite the protection of convoys, and how it threatened our food supplies and restricted the import of raw materials for the war effort. As a child I was not as much aware of the wider implications as the adults might have been, but the nation could never see the whole picture, only the gloss put on it by government propaganda to maintain morale. Gains and losses were acknowledged, and such was the skill of ministerial manipulation of information that we accepted that we were being told the truth. My parents were very loyal to the government and convinced of the veracity of the official interpretation of events as published in news bulletins. I never heard them express any scepticism.

Within a few months, the impact of the Battle of the Atlantic began to be felt in Britain; food rationing began. Until the end of 1939 we could buy what we needed as we always had done and, in our village, life for most people had been comfortable but simple. The nation was allowed to enjoy Christmas, but on 28 December[7] meat was rationed and on 8 January, 1940 more general rationing was introduced. From that time onward we became accustomed to increasing restrictions as allowances of rationed goods became smaller through the years, reflecting the success of the Germans' transatlantic naval campaign. In the village we were better placed than people in cities because we had our large vegetable gardens, our poultry, our fruit trees and soft fruit in season. People with sufficient space were allowed to keep one pig a year and kill it under licence. What I can't understand, in retrospect, is what ordinary householders did with all the meat, because we had no domestic refrigerators and no means of keeping it other than by salting it. Local farmers were always ready to do a favour for a friend: my father never went without his morning bacon, even if it was home cured and very fatty, and some of the juiciest pork I ever tasted was a choice piece of Mr

---

[7] Rationing: *Chronology,* 23-26.

and Mrs Brigham's Susie, though I admit to shedding a tear at her demise and I missed her cheerful grunt of greeting when I went to see her in the shed at the bottom of their garden. Food shortages did make an impact: we had our ordinary rations, which were small, particularly of imported goods such as tea; we didn't see an orange or a banana until shortly before the end of the war, but when goods were in short supply their fair distribution was controlled by a flexible points system whereby the Ministry of Food adjusted their points value according to availability.

By the end of 1939, then, the German U-boats and surface warships were seriously damaging transatlantic convoys and threatening fundamental supplies of food and materials essential to the war effort and the Allies had no effective answer to it. Resulting shortages came gradually and we grew accustomed to them. There was a different attitude of mind: you accepted what happened and didn't grumble. 'Don't you know there's a war on?' became a catch-phrase.

Other differences I remember clearly are those that affected school life and represented changes in priorities, the emergence of a different mentality. Drama was regarded as trivial in wartime, so the dramatic society was abandoned. School cadet corps were started for the older boys; on Fridays, in readiness for after-school meetings, their members wore the uniforms of the armed forces instead of coming to school dressed as Boy Scouts. Very mature and impressive they looked to the admiring girls, who had no equivalent and still wore their Girl Guide uniforms and worked for badges. Armistice Day, 11 November, lost its significance. Before the war the grammar school had maintained a tradition begun after the First World War: the whole school paraded in a crocodile down Knaresborough High Street for an Armistice service in the Parish Church, observing the two-minute silence at 11 o'clock. This was a solemn occasion and we walked smartly and quietly through the town. I had been proud of being watched by those out on the streets and, influenced by my father's attitude, felt that the parade represented something significant. Its absence, in 1939, was like mourning, a feeling that all the sacrifice it represented had been in vain.

Soon after the war began, the younger men on the staff were called up for service in the armed forces. Charlie Walker, the chemistry master, who was our form teacher that year, went into the RAF. He was very popular, always referred to by the pupils as 'Johnny Walker' ('born 1820, still going strong' in the words of the whisky advert). He was replaced by Mrs Kettlewood, a widow, a tiny woman in her forties with a daughter at the Castle Yard School. She was gentle and eager to please, and we liked her, but we took advantage of the fact that she was no disciplinarian, and noted with salacious pleasure and comment over the years the fact that she blushed and smiled a lot in the presence of Mr Street, the history teacher, with whom she held long conversations in the corridors accompanied by what we interpreted as adoring glances. The second loss to the staff was Mr Baggott, who had been our form teacher when he joined the staff the previous year. A conscientious objector on religious grounds, he stayed in Knaresborough and worked in a market garden throughout the war. Sometimes, when we were going to or from school, we would see him on his bicycle dressed for work and he always smiled at and spoke to the pupils he knew. He looked much happier than he had done in front of a class, where we had regarded him as humourless and bad-tempered. Mr Walker returned to the school after the war and stayed there until he retired. Apart from Mr Whellock, who taught junior sciences and also left, the other men on the staff had been there for some years and were above military age. For women, teaching was a reserved occupation, a factor which influenced my choice later.

In all these ways life took on different dimensions and we became used to change and uncertainty. On another level it was much the same: school, with the eternal grind of tests and 'monthly marks', the system whereby we were graded regularly for achievement; the morning boiled egg for breakfast and walk to the bus; the weary wait in the Tudor Cafe doorway for the bus to come jolting over the cobbled market place at night; the sickly journey home; the trail to the other end of the village at twenty-past five with an empty stomach and a satchel full of books. One joy was that double summer time was introduced, so that in the longest days it didn't get dark during waking hours. I loved the dewy morning coolness deep in my lungs as I went for the bus and, when I was older, the leisurely late evening walks round the lanes, returning in the mild, scented air and fading light as the face of the church clock showed eleven. Church bells were silenced by law; their tolling would signify a national emergency. My father could no longer ring the school bell, or even a hand-bell in the school yard, since a hand-bell was rung in the village as an air raid warning.

CHAPTER XI

Wartime: a way of life

During 1940, as throughout the war, international events and their repercussions on British life were known to our family mainly from news bulletins on the wireless. We switched on early in the mornings to see what the night had brought, caught the lunch-time news if we were around, and came together by the fireside in the evenings to listen to our favourite programmes and to hear the latest news before bedtime. The names and voices of the news-readers became familiar; Alvar Liddell and Bruce Belfrage were regular favourites. When there was anything momentous to report, the news was often read by John Snagge, whose portentous tones still echo in my mind as synonymous with crises. It was the first time the BBC had broken the convention that its news-readers should be anonymous, a measure to ensure the authenticity of the source,

This was where we learned of the expansion of war zones; of the German invasion of Norway and Denmark on 7 April, 1940, of the damaging and escape as they returned from Norway, of the notorious German battle cruisers, *Scharnhorst* and *Gneisenau*, which regularly wreaked havoc amongst our merchant fleet. There were many encounters with these notoriously destructive vessels. Unknown to us at the time the Whitleys from our local stations were taking an active part in this harassment and they, joined by the new four-engined Halifaxes which came to Linton-on-Ouse in November 1940, continued over the next year or more to take part in attacks on the harbours in which the enemy took refuge. When the first four-engined bombers were seen in our sky we used to gaze at them in astonishment; they seemed so large compared with the aircraft we had become accustomed to which, as well as the Whitleys, included fighters – Hurricanes and Spitfires. It was in order to accommodate these larger aircraft that there had been such a push to complete construction of the longer runways which had been unfinished at the beginning of the war. The Halifaxes soon became part of the background once they were operational in the New Year.

My mother and I still found Linton aerodrome an attractive focus for our cycle rides. After crossing Aldwark Bridge we turned right, where the road to Linton-on-Ouse followed a strip of woodland alongside which banks of wild strawberries grew. It was exciting to watch the aircraft taking off and landing, particularly as they crossed the open road. A simple notice warned passers-by to beware of low-flying aircraft; if we heard and saw one coming we stood back to watch while it flew over the dip in the road, neatly clearing the hedgerows. Under the government's 1935 plan to expand the nation's air defences the aerodrome had been built on prime farmland against local opposition and opened on 13 May, 1937, the month of King George VI's coronation. Its first commander was Air Commodore A.T. Harris, later Marshall of the Royal Air Force, Sir Arthur ('Bomber') Harris, Chief of Bomber Command.[8]

From 1938 onwards we had become accustomed to the presence of increased traffic through the village as lorries carried sand and gravel from the quarry at Marton-cum-Grafton to build the longer runways necessary for a viable night bomber force, which was the intended role of the chain of airfields being constructed down the eastern side of the country. These runways were incomplete in 1939 and traffic through the village increased with the need to finish them quickly. When British strategy concentrated increasingly on the destruction of the German war machine and attempted to demoralize its civilian population by intensive bombing, we witnessed the massing of these manned instruments of war and felt to be at the heart of the campaign.

---

[8] Peter D. Mason, *Wings over Linton (Mk II), The History of the Royal Air Force Linton-on-Ouse (1937-1997)* (Wetherby: A1 Press, 1994), 4.

The international dimension of the war largely passed me by; my attention was focused on anything that impinged on our daily lives, such as RAF activity, or affected our own country, such as Chamberlain's resignation as Prime Minister on 10 May 1940, and his replacement by Winston Churchill. He immediately formed an all-party cabinet and that same night, despite Germany's numerical superiority in the air, began a bombing offensive over Germany with a raid by thirty-six bombers on Monchengladbach. Meanwhile, the Allied forces in France were no match for the German armies and the British were retreating towards Dunkirk. The order for evacuation was given on 26 May and the next few days provided high drama, with stories of fishermen and owners of small pleasure boats crossing the English Channel to take part in the rescue of British troops, culminating on 4 June with Churchill's famous speech, '...we shall fight them on the beaches...'[9] in anticipation of the fall of France, which would leave Britain as the last European opponent of Hitler and vulnerable to immediate invasion.

The account of these events for the British public, like all knowledge of the progress of the war, was controlled by the Foreign Office through the Ministry of Information, whose unenviable task was to avoid disheartening the British people while providing a credibly realistic assessment of the situation. The BBC, working within official guidelines, provided news bulletins which emphasized heroic rescue missions and minimized the potential impact of the defeat, while giving sombre statistics which discouraged false hopes. Throughout the war, a few pioneer BBC correspondents such as Frank Gillard sent vivid eye-witness dispatches from all the major fronts, a new development in broadcasting, but these were always subject to official oversight and censorship.

---

[9] Churchill's speeches are readily available and can be listened to on line and as CDs. Also worth reading is Peter Barnard, *We interrupt this programme: Twenty stories that marked the century* (London: BBC publication, 1999).

Most of the statistics surrounding the Dunkirk retreat meant little to me, but I remember the quickened heart-beat and excitement of following every news bulletin, and the dread that underlay the ordinary comings and goings of daily life as I began to realize that the country was in a uniquely difficult and dangerous position. This awareness, like butterflies in the stomach that wouldn't go away, lurked in the background of my everyday activities, making them seem unreal, temporary. We were waiting: it seemed inevitable that Britain would be invaded and I could not visualize what horrors that would entail, and what changes might take place within a few short weeks, but my imagination played around various possibilities and succeeded only in creating imponderable fear.

On 11 June the French government moved to Tours and on 14 June the Germans entered Paris. On 17 June, Churchill made his 'finest hour' speech. My parents and I listened intently whenever he spoke to the nation. His rhetoric was heart-warming and reassuring: of course we wouldn't be defeated; after all, we believed, our cause was just; right was on our side and so, needless to say, was God. On 22 June, 1940 France signed an armistice with Germany.

Another name soon became familiar, that of Brigadier-General Charles de Gaulle who, on 28 June, was recognized by Britain as leader of the Free French. He broadcast regularly from London to the French people, encouraging them to continue the fight in whatever way they could. Because I was learning French he came to have a higher profile for me than might otherwise have been the case; as our knowledge of the language increased we were encouraged to listen to his broadcasts, a challenge which I found difficult, since French spoken by a native sounded very different from the language as taught by English people speaking relatively slowly. Throughout the war years the radio provided our only experience of French spoken by a native speaker; it is hard to realize now that, despite my eventual command of the written language, love of the meticulous craft of translation and of reading French literature, I had no chance to speak French with French people until we went to Paris in the 1970s. By then I already had a hearing problem and, although the French people we encountered understood my carefully prepared requests, I could make little of their part of a conversation, even at the level of simple shopping.

I didn't fully understand the implications of the fall of France, but the generalized dread that underlay the knowledge that we were at war became more acute at certain times, and this was one of those occasions. In memory I can still hear an echo of the portentous tones of Churchill's rhetoric on 14 July:

> Should the invader come to Britain there will be no placid lying down of the people in submission. We shall defend every village, every town, every city. The vast mass of London itself, fought street by street, could easily devour an entire hostile army and we would rather see London laid in ruins and ashes than that it should be tamely and abjectly enslaved.

Such a solemn promise frightened me; I imagined the battle for freedom being fought in Great Ouseburn and the familiar villages in our neighbourhood, in Boroughbridge and Knaresborough, and tried to accept that this could become the reality.

The weeks passed and the feared invasion did not take place. The summer holiday of 1940 was spent at home, like the next five. We didn't know then that the timetable laid down by Hitler for the invasion of Britain involved escalating air attacks and an invasion date eventually postponed until September, and that the air offensive making the daily headlines was to be its first stage.[10] Early in August Hitler had ordered the destruction of the RAF, and the British aircraft industry, which was working at full capacity to reduce the gap between Britain's fighter capability and that of Germany. On 15 August, for example, the Germans flew more than 2,000 sorties over south-east England and 1,700 the following day, and all three groups of Fighter Command were deployed against them for the first time. Meanwhile, Bomber

---

[10] Information about the Battle of Britain, the bombing of London and the abandonment of Hitler's invasion plans, *Chronology,* 44-49.

Command was attacking targets in Germany and further afield, including Turin, in Italy, where German fighter planes were manufactured. By 19 August the use of radar by the British was enabling them to confuse the German fighters and concentrate their own fighters where they would have the greatest chance of success. On 20 August Churchill made his famous speech praising the achievements of Fighter Command: 'Never in the field of human conflict was so much owed by so many to so few.'

On 24 August a German bomber lost course and off-loaded its bombs on London, an event which resulted in Churchill's ordering reprisals on Berlin, another operation in which the Yorkshire squadrons of Whitleys were involved.[11] This, in turn, led Hitler to order an air assault on London, with 60 tons of bombs dropped on the night of 5 September and more than 900 bombers attacking the city on 7 September. On 15 September, the day which would be known as 'Battle of Britain Day', the RAF used all its fighters for the first time, destroying 56 German aircraft, almost a quarter of their force, for the loss of 26 British planes. This convinced the Germans that they had failed to gain control of the skies, and the invasion plan was abandoned. Losses on both sides were heavy and their propaganda for the public minimized their seriousness. The BBC's regular news bulletins gave statistics of German aircraft destroyed and numbers of our fighters missing; reports of raids over Germany listed numbers missing, but these gave no impression of the overall pattern. By the end of September the Luftwaffe had delivered more than 6,000 tons of explosive bombs and 8,500 tons of incendiaries on London. Hitler's strategy changed, concentrating on night attacks. The port of Liverpool was attacked on 11 October and Coventry was subjected to a devastating attack on 14 November which reduced much of it to rubble and severely damaged the cathedral. On 16 November, in reprisal for the attack on Coventry, Mannheim was selected as a particular target; Berlin, Hamburg, Bremen and other cities in

---

[11] Wadsworth, *Heroes*, 34-5.

Germany and the occupied countries were also bombed. As we listened to news of retaliation such as this we were gratified that the enemy were paying the price in good measure for what had been done to our own cities.

From December, 1940, the four-engined Halifax bombers, already based at Leeming and newly introduced at Linton, increasingly became part of our regular sky-scape along with the familiar Whitleys and Wellingtons and some Spitfires and Hurricanes. There was always aerial activity as routine testing took place, new crews had to be familiarized with their planes, and squadrons were moved around from one airfield to another, including the smaller bases gradually being brought into commission. Anti-aircraft batteries and searchlight units had been set, well camouflaged, in open country near the airfields and searchlights routinely criss-crossed the night sky. We found them reassuring throughout the war, a symbol of watchfulness, gently illuminating the cloud cover on dark nights with their own characteristic beauty, or intensely, restlessly probing the darkness when they were all switched on during an alert.

The Ministry of Information was faced with a difficult but crucial task in trying to maintain national morale when Germany was imposing a heavy blockade on supply shipping in the Channel and throwing all its resources into the air attack. As bombing campaigns escalated, the appalling damage by both sides to Europe's cultural heritage, the suffering of civilians and the toll of the lives of young men in their late teens and early twenties could have been inferred by interpreting statistics, but the public had no knowledge of what was being revealed by the aerial photographs of destruction taken for military purposes; these are now on display in museums and shock the visitor into realization of the reality. We accepted the bulletins which were released to the media after they had been carefully prepared with the official gloss put on events by the government. In reality the bombing campaign on industrial targets in Germany and Italy during November and December 1940 was relentless.

From the point of view of a young listener, avid for sensational news, the Battle of Britain was an exciting daily contest, giving the impression that our brave airmen were fighting their way to victory against the odds. We were not in the part of the country where the action was taking place, but the statistics published daily and the dramatic photographs in newspapers reduced the devastating loss of men and machines to an overall impression that the enemy's losses were much greater than ours and that we were winning the contest. What brought the reality to our village was the news that Dr Benson's elder son, Noel, a fighter pilot, had been killed in action. I only knew him as a young man in smart clothing driving through the village with his younger brother in an open-topped sports car, probably on their way to see their friends, the Machins, who lived near Cattal.

Significant events charting the international situation were always in the background as we waited for the latest bulletins, but other considerations made more impact on our daily lives. Shortly after rationing was introduced in 1940, my father was informed that he must arrange for school dinners to be available at a cost of fourpence for a two-course meal. Families who couldn't afford to pay would be given free meals, an essential arrangement in a community where many families had three or more children aged between five and thirteen at school. The West Riding would pay the wages of a cook and helper and provide some basic essentials, in accordance with government policy for catering establishments; the other ingredients must be supplied locally and paid for out of income. Mrs Smith, the caretaker, was keen to do the cooking, but unwilling to take further responsibility. Mrs Thirkill was appointed as helper. My mother eagerly took on the challenge of providing varied menus within the budget allowed. I was not sufficiently involved to know whether there was a coupon system for rationed goods, but many unrationed ingredients were readily available. Potatoes could be supplied by the sackful by local farmers, and turnips were very cheap. Fruit and vegetables could be provided by the greengrocer who came to the village from Boroughbridge, but most seasonal vegetables could be grown in the school garden. My father took over the garden of what had been the Parkers' house across the road from the school, since the house now stood empty and the unused garden with its fruit bushes was becoming overgrown. Educational priorities were adjusted and in the gardening season the senior boys and girls spent a great deal of time in the afternoons learning the practicalities of growing food for their dinners.

This new venture was probably the most significant change in my life resulting from the war. My mother ordered what was needed from local tradesmen and managed the allowances from the West Riding; for example we had a huge flour bin in the corner of the kitchen. She kept the accounts, devised menus and calculated weights and measures; every day after school she weighed out ingredients for the next day's meal and we carried them through into the kitchen which had been set up in the 'cod liver oil room'. A rumbling mechanical potato peeler and a vast iron kitchen range similar to an 'Aga', with hot-plates and a large oven, had been installed there, along with stout work tables, and Mrs Smith, always ready to chat, came in to make her own preparations for the following day.

Wednesday's menu is firmly fixed in my mind, because the grammar school had slightly longer and occasionally different holidays and when I was at home my meal, too, was brought into the house. We had roast mutton, with Yorkshire pudding, crisp roast potatoes cooked in the dripping from the meat, creamy mashed potato, and whatever vegetable was in season; the thickened gravy was made from the drainings of the joint. I have never since tasted meat quite like this generous slice from the middle of a large leg of mutton; it was lean and tender and had a rich, full flavour which 'lamb' cannot match. Willy Barrit, who had set up business in Little Ouseburn and supplied all the meat for school dinners, brought the joint to the house on Tuesday evenings. Typically, it cost 17s.6d. and was sufficient to serve everybody. Wednesday's pudding was always baked apple sponge and custard. My parents and I were fortunate that five main meals of the week were available outside our personal rations. Many other people throughout the country were in a similar position, having access to works canteens or government-aided British Restaurants offering inexpensive cooked meals.

The West Riding provided extra sugar, above the usual allowance, for jam-making, in line with the small extra seasonal ration permitted to the general public for this purpose. We already had a large brass pan, of the kind traditionally hung over kitchen fires, which my father had bought at a village sale some years previously and which my mother always used to make our own jam. It just fitted over one burner of the paraffin stove. Initially, in order to build up the supply we needed, the children were asked to bring empty jam jars to school, and my mother and I made jams and jellies from everything available – raspberries and gooseberries, rhubarb and redcurrants, damsons and apples. When the hedgerows were full of ripe blackberries and crab apples, we went out into the lanes and fields to gather them and the children were encouraged to do the same, so we made bramble and apple jelly with the autumn bounty.

In a strenuous life, with its routine bus journey to school, tedious, weary return at the end of the day, and the daily grind of school work and homework, it was wonderfully relaxing to go out into the garden and gather fruit in its season: thick, tender rhubarb; redcurrants ripened to glowing perfection, hanging in clusters; raspberries, aromatic in the warm evening sun; gooseberries, the surplus young green thinnings for pies in spring and the ripe, translucent green and red ones ideal for jam. It was refreshing to squelch the sweet flesh and seeds of the largest, ripest ones into my mouth, rejecting the rough, sour skins. In autumn there was the excitement of picking apples and damsons. Parkers' garden had a lovely old tree which bore fine crops of pin damsons, the tangy fruit too sharp to enjoy raw, but perfect for stewing and for richly flavoured jam. My mother and I took the step-ladder to reach some of the higher ones and carried baskets full of fruit across the road. Nothing was more satisfying than gathering in our harvest and turning it into aromatic sweetness, watching the bubbling pan, breathing in the heady aroma of fruit. Blackberries always smelt just that little bit more enticing than the taste of the finished jelly. We made well over a hundred jars of preserves every season, ensuring that jam roly-poly pudding featured regularly on the menu for school meals and there was ample jam for rice, sago and semolina puddings throughout the year. For both of us it was pleasurable, companionable and satisfying and we took a pride in getting 'pound for pound' from the fruit and sugar, and a firm set. We also made chutney from unripe gooseberries, green tomatoes and apples, to serve with meat. When my mother had to return to teaching in 1943 this work still went on at the end of the day and at weekends.

There was one exception to this success story. One batch of crab-apple jelly refused to set at the critical point where you can catch the boiling mixture without turning it to a saturated solution and losing bulk and flavour. My mother was determined to make it set and kept on boiling and testing it without apparent success until it was dark, thick and syrupy. In disgust she turned it out into greased shallow baking trays, where it cooled into the most delicious gooey, stretchy toffee we'd ever tasted. To my sorrow, she never repeated the experiment.

From my point of view the regular harvesting of whatever was in season was sheer delight; I loved the feeling of providing from nature's store. I'd always enjoyed the whole concept of harvest, even collecting twigs for kindling. It satisfied some basic urge to forage for what was there in abundance and preserve it for the pleasure of eating what had been grown, picked or created from the produce. Autumn, particularly, was rich with the smell of ripe fruit as well as the glory of turning leaves. The gathering instinct of the hunter-gatherers is still as strong in me as it ever was; a supermarket trolley, though a poor substitute, brings a similar welcome opportunity to urban life, and I should be sad if I became too frail to pick raspberries and blackcurrants in my son-in-law's fruit and vegetable garden in Nidderdale.

In these ways, then, wartime enhanced my love of the garden, the countryside and the passing seasons, and increased the satisfaction that I'd always gained from being out of doors in the midst of it all and carrying home fresh produce available for the picking. Everyday life focused on what had always been a feature of country living – the provision of food from the land by careful husbandry and the willing expenditure of time. What applied to food applied equally to clothing. The government devised appropriate slogans: 'Dig for victory', 'Make do and mend'. The meagre allowance of clothing coupons ensured that my mother had to do even more assiduously what she had always done by reason of limited resources and family tradition and I learned from her.

We were well placed to supplement our rations and maintain our poultry. There was no shortage of corn from the farmers, though officially they were not supposed to sell it, and we used left-over scraps from school dinners and boiled potatoes to mix in with commercial poultry mash for the evening feed. When there was a glut of eggs in spring and summer we put the spare ones into a bucket of 'water glass' to preserve them. It gradually thickened round them into a white, slushy solid, from which we dug them out and rinsed them as required during the winter when the hens were not in lay. They were fine for baking, could be fried or scrambled and still tasted acceptable when there was nothing fresher, but they cracked if you boiled them.

Throughout the war years Uncle Ernest, who worked for a small cooperative grocery firm, visited us frequently for day trips, carrying a small, shabby blue case. It contained two or three bags of sugar and packets of tea, and a pound or two of butter that was often past its best. Butter went rancid relatively quickly before people had refrigerators, but its slightly stale flavour was partly disguised and not too unpleasant in cakes. We never questioned the origins of this 'black market' extra and, in return, filled the case carefully with a couple of dozen fresh eggs wrapped in newspaper for him to take home for himself and Uncle Harry. Sometimes the two of them came for the weekend. Uncle Harry was unhappy in his job because the fine timber for furniture making was no longer imported from abroad and there were close restrictions on what could be made. Consequently, the firm he had worked for as a skilled cabinet-maker went out of business quite early in the war. He then went to work in a factory making 'utility' furniture instead of the beautifully crafted veneered bedroom and dining suites he had always made, and he spent his days unfulfilled at a lathe or knocking together pre-cut units to make the prescribed, simple mass-produced products. The 'utility' mark became familiar on such products as clothing and bed linen, too. It guaranteed a basic, adequate product at a reasonable price, using materials which the country could afford and obtain.

As the autumn of 1940 gave way to one of the two worst winters I can remember, we had another group of evacuees in the village, mothers with babies and young children and a few unaccompanied older children from the bomb-damaged areas of the east end of London. Accustomed to city life, they found winter in our village intolerably hard. One poor woman with two young children was placed in Starra Cottage, which had stood empty for months. It was damp, with paper peeling off the walls, outdoor toilet facilities, and no means of heating water apart from in a pan on the fire. Others were billeted on local people; Mr and Mrs Smith took in a mother with a young baby and found it difficult to be reconciled to what they saw as a very different culture, with poor standards of personal hygiene compared with their own. Country people, whose work involved animals and the farmyard, understood the need to be clean and careful; they took a pride in such fundamentals, in spite of the simplicity of their cottages and lack of amenities.

January and February of 1941 saw one of the two heaviest snowfalls I was ever to experience in that area, blown on an icy wind. Drifts were several feet deep at the bottom of the village and a team from the army came to dig out a path between Great Ouseburn and the fish-pond bridge. The village itself was cleared adequately by the usual horse-drawn snow ploughs, but my mother and I went for walks down to the bridge, just for the fun of walking between the walls of snow. The school bus came as regularly as possible, the driver armed with a spade and sacks which he would spread in front of the tyres to aid the spinning wheels when it ran into packed ice or the curls of newly drifting snow blown off the fields by the wind. The drifts were spectacularly beautiful, transforming the landscape as the snow was sculpted by the hedgerows. The snow ploughs did what they could to keep the lanes accessible, but there was no salt and sand to spread on them. Whenever the bus came to a halt, or skidded off the narrow, cleared area we all cheered, hoping it might slide into a ditch. When we eventually arrived in Knaresborough it was exciting to trudge down the snow-packed pavements from the bus stop in the cobbled market place and arrive at school unavoidably late, and miss assembly and part of the first lesson. Occasionally, after a fresh snowfall, we waited in vain for the bus to arrive and returned gleefully home.

After experiencing such conditions during the early months of 1941, by which time German air raids on London had eased considerably, the evacuees soon decided they would prefer to take their chance at home rather than spend the rest of the winter in a bleak northern village. The costly onslaught had failed to provide the Germans with an opening for invasion or break British morale, and Hitler's attention had turned to Eastern Europe.

Gradually the village scene was changing. Mrs Tunstill no longer lived in Moat Hall, which was commandeered to provide a hostel for the Women's Land Army. Land girls worked on the local farms and socialized in the village pubs in the evenings, particularly the one nearest to our house, the *Three Horse Shoes*, breaking the perception that the only women who drank regularly in a pub were the few local girls of dubious reputation with an eye for the men; friends of the landlord's wife at the *Bay Horse*, for example, sat with her in the saloon away from the uninhibited talk of farmers and farm labourers. The other group who congregated in the *Three Horse Shoes* were RAF men from Linton-on-Ouse, many of them ground staff, who cycled to Great Ouseburn in preference to patronizing the local pubs or the *Alice Hawthorne* at Nun Monkton favoured by most officers and air crew. Obviously, it had attractions.

The local airfields attracted enemy attention from time to time, contributing to the number of air raid warnings that disturbed our nights. They failed to put any of the stations out of action, but on one occasion in 1941 the station commander was killed when leading a team of fire fighters to deal with an incendiary raid on Linton.[12] On another occasion several bombs dropped in a field near the river when a German aircraft had

---

[12] Wadsworth, *Heroes*, 140. No date is given for the attack in which G/C Garroway was killed.

failed to hit Aldwark Bridge and achieve its objective, to cut the supply route between Grafton quarry and the ongoing building work at Linton. We went down to look at the craters, which appeared small and inoffensive in a field, but would have been effective in a direct hit on such a fragile structure as the bridge. It would not have been difficult for the Germans to know where the airfields were from their own observations, but there was a great deal of government publicity to make people aware that any scrap of sensitive information could help an enemy agent: 'Careless Talk Costs Lives' was one slogan on the Ministry's posters.

By 1941 a few married RAF men had found lodgings in the village; some were air crew, others were ground staff. Jack Robinson and his wife took in Jack and May Lovegrove, a childless couple in their mid-thirties. He was a Leading Aircraftsman involved with maintenance of the bombers. We became very friendly with Jack, who had been a chauffeur in Brighton before he was called up for national service; May had been in hotel work. My Dad always hated driving and Jack was happy to drive the car whenever we wanted to use our petrol ration to go into town. May went along as well and enjoyed these occasions which enabled her to get out of the village. In retrospect, I think she was very bored; there was no opportunity for her to work, apart from seasonal potato-picking. Jack enjoyed coming across in the evenings to tinker with the car and chat to all of us. Inevitably I had a crush on this good-looking man in uniform and, whenever maths became particularly obscure, I would gaze up into the corner of the room and visualize his face, or draw ornate versions of JWL in my jotter.

The sound of aircraft began to dominate our evenings as night bombing of Germany increased after the Battle of Britain. Halifaxes were appearing in larger numbers, a second squadron being based at Linton-on-Ouse by April 1941, and we became aware of a lot more daytime movement of aircraft. According to later accounts this was the period when aircrews were becoming more international and there was considerable movement of men and squadrons between local airfields as new facilities became available and deployment was adjusted to losses: Canadians, together with some French and British crew members, were manning the Halifaxes. We noted where the raids had taken place when we listened to the news. On 8 May, 1941, for example, the RAF launched an attack by 359 bombers on Hamburg and Bremen and this would be one of many occasions when we were sure that 'our' planes had been involved.[13]

For me there was a certain poignancy in watching them, a vicarious emotional investment in the popular song, 'Silver wings in the moonlight' and a naively sentimental acceptance of the bond between man and machine:

> Silver wings in the moonlight, flying high up above,
> While I'm patiently waiting, please take care of my love…
> If you love him like I do, take him safely, and then
> Silver wings in the moonlight, bring him homeward again.

Caught up in mindless hatred of the enemy and assurance of the justice of our cause, I had no concept of the cost in young lives of intelligent and highly trained men, many of them only four or five years older than me, the reality hidden by the bland announcements of 'successful' raids, followed by a statement of the number of aircraft missing. As far as I was concerned this was giving the Germans what they deserved for bombing our cities. If we woke in the night and heard damaged planes faltering as they returned, we would listen apprehensively and hope they would not crash. There was a popular song for that situation, too:

> Coming in on a wing and a prayer;
> Coming in on a wing and a prayer.
> Though we've one motor gone,
> We can still carry on,
> Coming in on a wing and a prayer.

---

[13] This raid and the reprisal raids on British airfields and the Rolls-Royce factory in the Midlands, together with the account of Hess's landing in Scotland, *Chronology*, 69.

We had little true impression of the horrific experiences and suffering underlying those words as we watched them leaving and heard them passing overhead again in the early hours. The grim drama being played out on the neighbouring airfields, so close and yet so remote from the lives we lived, was reduced in our minds to the revving and take-off, the awesome sight of the squadrons in the air, the news of targets successfully attacked and the final bald statistic, '[number] of our aircraft are missing'.

On 10 May, 1941 a strange incident was reported on the radio, the independent flight to Scotland of Rudolf Hess, deputy leader of Hitler's Nazi Party, apparently to make contact with a former acquaintance, the Duke of Hamilton, in the mistaken belief that there was a strong anti-Churchill group in Britain who would work with Germany. He was interned for the duration of the war, then transferred to Spandau prison in Berlin where later he committed suicide. This event is associated in my mind with an inexplicable occurrence at about the same time.

It has not reached the history books, but we were involved in it. One bright morning when the orchard trees were in blossom we were awakened by the ringing of our front door bell and the presence on our doorstep of army officers, who announced that they were commandeering a room in the house as their headquarters: a number of empty German parachutes had been discovered in orchards in the locality and this could be a preliminary to the anticipated invasion. It seemed likely that German troops were at large in the neighbourhood. I was absolutely terrified and overwhelmed by a sense of unreality: this was the nightmare coming true. By the end of the day the officers had decided that these were just empty parachutes dropped by the Germans, and assumed that they were part of a terror campaign to demoralize the British people. They departed as briskly as they had come and we relaxed. The incident reached the news bulletins briefly: it had apparently occurred in several places in the north of the country. On 22 June, 1941 Hitler invaded Russia and the invasion threat to Britain was finally over.

The campaign against the four German 'capital' warships, *Scharnhorst, Gneisenau, Prinz Eugen* and *Bismarck,* which together had the potentiality to carry out a successful blockade of essential supplies to Britain, was ongoing for almost three years. This dangerous 'hide and seek' was costly, and was part of the operational life of our local stations. The aim was to destroy them or at least to damage them sufficiently to keep them confined to the ports in which they took refuge or were being repaired. One engagement in which our local aircraft took part was that of the night of 24 July 1941 when 15 Halifaxes from Linton-on-Ouse were sent to attack the Scharnhorst at La Pallice, while local Blenheims were attacking the Gneisenau and Prinz Eugen at Brest. Of the fifteen Halifaxes, five were shot down and all the rest were damaged by fighters.[14] This was just one example of the cost of this battle in men and machines to keep these deadly ships away from the Atlantic and the English Channel.

Meanwhile, between 1940 and 1941, the campaign in North and East Africa had been prominent in the news. Italy had declared war on Britain and France on 10 June, 1940 and had concentrated her large, but comparatively ill-trained and badly equipped forces in areas around the Mediterranean. They had attacked the South of France before the surrender, and moved from Abyssinia into Kenya and British Somaliland. By mid-September, 1940 the Italians were achieving some success against weak British forces in North Africa, but they lacked experience and an overall understanding of strategy.[15] By November and December, the strengthening of British forces led to widespread retreat of the Italians and, by 6 January, 1941, the British began the encirclement of Tobruk in which a large Italian force was then based. When the garrison surrendered on 22 January more than 27,000 prisoners were taken.

---

[14] Jackson, *Before the Storm*, 150

[15] Comments regarding Italian occupation of Sollum on the African coast, *Chronology* 47.

These events ultimately affected life in our village. The former workhouse now stood empty, having been phased out gradually as a village institution during the 1930s. It was opened as a prisoner-of-war camp to house Italian prisoners, who would work on the land. They were regarded by the farmers as pleasant men and willing workers; like the land girls, they became a familiar sight in the fields around the village in their prison uniform and could be seen at the windows and in the grounds of the workhouse as we walked by. When these men were repatriated after the capitulation of Italy, confirmed on 8 September, 1943, they were replaced by German prisoners, who remained until the end of the war. During the last few months, while awaiting repatriation, they were allowed to go for walks freely in the locality and even became friendly with a few local women. We never had any animosity towards these prisoners of war, because we knew that, somewhere in Germany or German-occupied territory, many of our own men also were sitting out the conflict.

My feelings were ambivalent, though I didn't analyze them at the time. I accepted the de-humanizing stereotypes of wartime, hating Hitler and 'the Germans' as the enemy who were destroying our cities and our shipping and killing our soldiers, and rejoiced when the bombers went to 'retaliate', but these Italians and the Germans who succeeded them were just men who happened to be on the other side, conscripted and caught up in conflict like many young British men and women. As a schoolgirl from a Yorkshire village, who had never been abroad, it fascinated me to think that these prisoners of war were working among our farmers, and that they spoke a different language. I used to look at them curiously, but it never occurred to me that, increasingly as policy changed, thousands of such people, men, women and children, were being killed every night by the young men who flew those aircraft passing overhead. I didn't seriously contemplate the moral issues associated with widespread bombing of civilian targets until, nearly fifty years after these events, we stayed on a number of occasions with a delightful family in Erfurt in the former East Germany after the Berlin Wall came down and when reconstruction was still in its early stages. Later still, we visited Dresden. I think these moral issues can never be resolved, as recent events in the Middle East illustrate only too plainly.

By the end of November, 1941 the daily news was coming mainly from three areas.[16] Italian forces finally surrendered in East Africa on the 28th, while the fighting in North Africa, which continued against Rommel and the German Afrika Corps, looked optimistic for the Allies. On the Russian front, the Germans were attempting a pincer movement on Moscow, with apparent success, but had yet to encounter the winter itself and the well-trained troops arriving from Siberia, who were experts in winter conditions. What still seemed peripheral to all this from our point of view was the regular news of the conflict between Japan and China. At the end of November, the Americans were attempting to persuade Japan, by promises of trade agreements, to withdraw from China and recognize Chiang Kai-shek. But the situation was about to change: America failed to realize the significance of Japanese naval movements noticed by the British in Borneo. On 7 December, 1941 came the news of the Japanese attack on Pearl Harbour,[17] followed swiftly by mutual declarations of war by Germany and America on 11 December and shortly afterwards by the arrival of members of the American forces in Britain.

These events were just a background to my daily life. I was much more immediately concerned about the pressures of my School Certificate year and anticipation of the change that would come the following July when most of our class would leave school. A few of us would choose our subjects for Higher School Certificate and return to join the prestigious Sixth Form and become prefects. My head resounded with sonorous lines from Tennyson's *Passing of Arthur* and *Henry IV, Part I*, French vocabulary and history notes. I drew floral diagrams and learned

---

[16] *Chronology*, 89-91.

[17] For events leading up to Pearl Harbour and an account of the attack, *Chronology*, 89-93.

about transpiration, respiration and photosynthesis and how to test for protein in peas, tried in vain to balance chemical equations, assiduously learned the current definition of an atom as a unit of matter which couldn't be divided, and took comfort from the fact that I could at least solve arithmetical problems, understand trigonometry and learn theorems, even if most of the things I could prove from looking at a geometrical diagram were not required to answer the question; anything beyond the most elementary algebra remained a mystery.

The atrocious winter weather which dominated the early weeks of 1942 effectively spoiled my chances of a distinction in art because the bus was always so excitingly late on Fridays that, to my joy, I missed a substantial part of the teaching in architecture which formed the first period of our double art lesson; this bored me, so I lacked the incentive to spend extra time studying the tedious drawings of capitals and columns and sequences of cathedral styles from the small illustrations and cramped text in our books. It was far more interesting to spend art homework time taking care over the drawing of twigs and flowers, and I even enjoyed designing half-drop patterns, the one exercise for which we were allowed to use paint. The school had no adequately equipped art room, because art, like music, was regarded as peripheral to real education; a classroom which was also the lower fifth form room, with people's books in the desks, was far too vulnerable to spills to allow the regular use of water and paint. When a particularly beautiful spring came, the winter's excitement faded and we concentrated on the serious work ahead.

CHAPTER XII

The later war years, 1942-1945

On 14 February, 1942 RAF Bomber Command received a directive to launch attacks which would damage enemy morale, particularly in the industrial areas, effectively, though only implicitly at this stage, freeing them from the instruction to avoid civilian targets. On 22 February, Air Marshall Arthur Harris was appointed Chief of RAF Bomber Command. His intended strategy was to use the air force to 'invade' Germany until ground forces could counter-attack in Europe later in the year.[18]

In March, a new shape began to dominate the skies above us, another large four-engined bomber, the Lancaster, which was being established at Linton and the other local aerodromes as part of this developing strategy. Though the Whitleys were still at Dishforth in February 1942 they were withdrawn from service shortly afterwards. From then onwards Halifaxes and Lancasters became the familiar night flyers, droning overhead laden with bombs, the image that dominates my memories of summer evenings. On 29 March they took part in a bombing raid on Lubeck, which was so successful that, in April, Hitler ordered a series of reprisals, the first of which was an attack on Exeter on 24 April, followed by an attack on Bath the following night.

I had a cold when the air raid warning sounded during the night of 29 April and large numbers of bombs could be heard exploding not very far away. With a streaming nose and sore throat I watched from my parents' bedroom window as the sky

---

[18] Appointment of 'Bomber' Harris, *Chronology*, 102 and *Heroes* 56-8.

over York became red with the fires started by incendiary bombs, and the dull thumping of high explosives continued. There had been occasional raids on York previously, but they had done very little damage. This was clearly of a different order and, it later transpired, was one of these reprisals targeting cathedral cities. Eventually things quietened down and we went back to bed when the all-clear sounded, though the fires were still burning brightly. To our relief, the familiar outline of the Minster could still be seen in the morning, standing out on the distant horizon of the flat landscape.

The raid had been successful in that York was a significant railway junction for the nationwide transport of materials necessary to the war effort. We later learned that the railway station had been very badly damaged. The Guildhall, also, had been virtually destroyed, along with St Martin's Church in Coney Street, and property in the surrounding part of the city, particularly the Bootham, Scarcroft and Acomb areas had been damaged. The Bar Convent and its school received a direct hit. A former air raid worker has described helping to get some of the nuns and pupils out through a coal chute in Nunnery Lane.[19] Poppleton Road School, familiar to us as we went into York along the Boroughbridge Road, had a large crater at its centre. The damage to the Leeman Road area around the railway and its associated offices was considerable. The suggestion was that the Minster, standing as it does in the heart of the Vale of York, provided the Luftwaffe with a good reference point from the air and, unlike Coventry, Manchester and Exeter Cathedrals, it was untouched. The warning had come too late for the air defence to be effective and later statistics revealed that 92 civilians had been killed and 204 injured, not to mention the number of people whose homes were badly damaged. We went into York a few days later to see for ourselves what had happened and were shocked by the destruction in the main target area.

---

[19] Van Wilson, *Rations, Raids and Romance: York in the Second World War* (York: York Archaeological Trust, 2008) .Chapter 6. This book is a fascinating collection of wartime reminiscences.

The summer term of 1942 saw the freedom of flexible attendance at school during the School Certificate examinations. Those of us who travelled from outlying rural districts had to spend the whole school day in Knaresborough because there were no alternative buses, but it was a pleasantly warm summer and we passed time very happily in the mornings or afternoons when we had no exam. Vera and Joan and I usually stayed together, and were sometimes joined by Doreen, who lived in Knaresborough. We often walked through the Castle Yard and down to Abbey Road. Our favourite pastime was to hire a punt and go on the river, even braving 'Cherry Deep', where only a foot of the pole projected from the water. We took turns in punting and became skilled in directing the punt. I rejoiced in the balance and grace involved in using the pole; it didn't worry me at all that I couldn't swim, but we were prudent and kept well away from the rapids. When we were hot and tired, with unused time to spend, we would tie up in the shade and chat and feel very grown-up and wicked as we shared a packet of cigarettes 'to keep off the flies'.

Our lunch hours were always spent out of school. We had decided in the fourth form that school dinners were dull and tasteless at the best, if not positively unpleasant, with over-cooked vegetables, heavy puddings and watery custard. Worse still, we sat at long tables, girls at one, boys at the other, supervised by members of staff, with grace before and after meals and complaints about the scraping of plates and mixing of jam into rice pudding. The caretaker's wife, Maud, a small, plump, unsmiling woman with a mass of chestnut hair, was the cook, and by lunchtime she was red in the face and even more out of temper than usual, mashing dry potatoes vigorously in the steamy kitchen with a tool that turned them out looking like piles of roundworms. A small group of us had been given permission to go to the Tudor Cafe in the cobbled market place every day instead of having school dinners. We sat in a particular corner upstairs and had a set two-course meal for half a crown a week, usually meat, roast and mashed potatoes, vegetables, delicious gravy, fish and chips on Fridays, followed by apple or treacle sponge or jam roly-poly, with thick custard, or a milk pudding. We would stroll round town after lunch and go back to school in time for the afternoon session. In 1942, after a morning exam, we sometimes spent part of the afternoon playing tennis or sitting in the sun. It was satisfying to savour the beginnings of the freedom and privilege that went with seniority.

September came; I was now sixteen and those of us who were joining the sixth form returned to school, eagerly anticipating the pleasures and privileges of our new status. We were given our prefects' badges, duties and timetables and the eight of us in lower sixth arts took our place at one of the two long tables in the library; the upper sixth occupied the other, though, of course, our use of the library in lesson times never coincided. As it happened, we never moved onto the other table, because only three people joined the arts sixth form the following year and they shared the parts of the English and history curriculum that we studied in our second year and had their own classes otherwise. The science sixth form were based in the labs, but they came into the library after lunch to socialize and play table tennis. Traditionally, in winter or on wet days, anyone who wished to do so could enjoy ballroom dancing during the lunch hour in the gym, where several people took turns in playing waltzes, quicksteps, foxtrots and some 'old-time' tunes on the piano. We were still more than happy to join in this activity, regardless of our seniority, particularly as the older boys were equally keen.

The central heating in the library was inadequate because of the area occupied by bookshelves, but we were allowed to light a fire in the old fireplace with its tiled surround and high mantelpiece. We collected kindling and a bucket of coal each morning from the boiler room, the exclusive kingdom of the morose caretaker, Albert, who would even smile sometimes as he handed over the bucket, despite the fact that he had the chore of cleaning out the ashes of the library and staff room fires when we'd all gone home.

French language lessons were most conveniently taught at the tables, but our enjoyment of English literature was enhanced by working our way through set texts with Mrs Beaumont and history of literature with Miss Sawdon, sitting in a friendly circle round a real fire whenever note-taking was not essential. If we all became pinker and a little less attentive as the lesson progressed, nobody suggested that we should return to the tables. When those of us who were studying history gathered in the men's long, narrow staff-room, redolent of tobacco, in the dark corner away from the small window, where their glowing fire warmed us gently, it was infinitely soothing to hear Mr Street's deep, mellifluous voice outlining the Treaty of Utrecht or the Peace of Westphalia and easier to drift into warm sleepiness than to contemplate the significance of what he was saying; we could rely on the notes that would come later to be sure of passing his regular tests and were mistakenly convinced that they were all we needed to know.

The real privilege and pleasure was to go into the headmaster's house for Latin lessons with Mrs Robinson, sitting around the table in the sunny dining room, with a fire in the hearth on dull, cold days. Three of us, who were hoping to go to university to read English, needed Latin at least to School Certificate level and preferably higher. It was important to reach the basic School Certificate level as quickly as possible and go on to Subsidiary level by our second year in the sixth form, because there was no option for an extra year at school. Under wartime regulations, students going to university or college to take an approved course must be eighteen or younger, the alternative being to go into the armed forces. In fact there were several sixteen and seventeen-year-olds among those who began their university course in 1944. We girls studying arts subjects gained our exemption by undertaking to become recognized students in training for teaching and had to promise to teach for at least two years after qualifying. If we had studied sciences we could have done the same, or equally well have applied for medicine, dentistry or agriculture. Boys were not allowed to take arts courses unless medically unfit, but could read maths and sciences, medicine, dentistry, metallurgy, agriculture and various engineering courses on condition that they continued to pass all their examinations throughout the course; failure to do so meant that they must go straight into the forces and complete their

175

studies after the war. At some point after I reached seventeen I had to register for national service. I filled in a form, but there were no further formalities as I was never called to an interview for the armed forces. Since farm labourers, unlike farmers, were not exempt from national service, several boys who had been my contemporaries in the village school went into the army or air force, as did some girls. I rather envied Edie Harland and Alice Bramley when they came home on leave in their uniforms.

A less extreme winter than the previous two gave way to the spring of 1943. At home the repetitive routine continued: weighing and measuring ingredients for school dinners; cutting and boiling potatoes for the poultry; growing and picking fruit and vegetables and, for me, the burden of homework increased. On fine Saturday afternoons that spring and summer I would cycle with my tennis racquet along the main road to the Aldborough junction, turn into the village and round the corner to Manor Farm, where Joan lived. Her Saturday job as the eldest girl of four was to scrub the dairy floor. When she had finished we walked along the road to Boroughbridge, to the town's tennis courts opposite the new modern school. The grass was worn and bumpy in places, but it made for exciting and unpredictable results; we met a group of boys and girls aged around fifteen to nineteen and wore our ageing tennis balls threadbare and our catgut racquet strings soft and wispy, but we had fun.

Then Joan and I went back to Manor Farm for tea and ham sandwiches and home-made cakes with lots of fresh cream, and I biked back in the early evening, knowing that darkness was several hours away. The quarry at Grafton had closed for the weekend; the farmers' field work was done; so I virtually had the high road to myself, and whizzed back at top speed with lengthening shadows and the panorama of the evening sky behind me. Sometimes I went the more winding, low road way from Aldborough, through Lower and Upper Dunsforth, enjoying the evening air, the scents changing with the passing of spring into summer: hawthorn, blossoming lime trees, wild roses and meadowsweet, the bitter smell of marshy ground drifting across the low-lying fields, and the pungent odour of cattle mooing a greeting or challenge through smoky breath near the hedges and field gates. As the dew fell, my feet in their open sandals would be cool on the pedals before I reached home.

The year was 1942-3, which saw the start of my friendship with the Riley family, who had originally farmed in the East Riding, and now lived in Prospect Farm on the other side of Church Lane from the vicarage. They had asked me to keep an eye on their elder daughter, Mary, who was going into the first form as I joined the sixth-form. I had an open invitation to visit them, particularly at weekends and during the holidays, and I formed a firm friendship with the whole family, who appealed to me as less drearily serious than my parents and made me feel unreservedly welcome.

Mrs Riley and her mother, Mrs Turner, ran the household, in which also lived Mrs Turner's two unmarried brothers who worked on the farm. I rarely saw them, but Mr Riley was always around for supper. Paula, who was only four when I first started visiting the house, tagged along with whatever Mary and I did. Mrs Riley, a vivacious thirty-six-year-old, was full of fun, and she and her mother, an equally vivacious sixty-some, always had time to chat and obviously enjoyed my company. Chatting was as much part of what we did as playing. Another regular visitor to the family was Vincent Reed, nicknamed 'Weedy' by Mary and Paula. He had a standing invitation to Sunday dinner and often came in the evenings. The four of us played ball or cricket or hide and seek in the farm yard and its buildings behind the house. In the winter evenings we played card games with Mrs Riley and Mrs Turner by the fireside in their comfortable, low-ceilinged sitting room, with its chandelier, table lamps and large mirror on the wall.

The highlight of their regular family routine was supper at the big table in the farm kitchen. Mrs Turner was a superb cook and there was no shortage of homemade bread and scones, freshly churned butter, jam and cream. There were always sandwiches of lean home-boiled ham, tangy with mustard, followed by a mouth-watering choice from a table laden with fruit pies and the lightest Victoria sandwich cakes I've ever eaten, filled with jam and whipped cream, coloured green or pink to appeal to Mary and Paula and cut into neat squares, rather larger than a mouthful, but not so big that you couldn't eat two or three. After supper, when the church clock, visible through their kitchen window on summer evenings, showed eleven, Vincent Reed would walk me down the village to the school gate, companionably arm in arm. The Rileys teased us about this, but he seemed to enjoy taking a 'young lady' home.

He was an interesting man, excellent company, a bachelor in his fifties, who had been born in Great Ouseburn and had lived with his mother until she died. His handwriting was a beautiful copper-plate, which he put to good effect as Parish Clerk, and he was an autodidact with a highly individual philosophy of life broadly based on theosophy. His response to the greeting, 'How are you?' was always the same: 'Very well, barring old age and poverty!' Though he obviously had adequate independent means for his own simple wants, he became the village road-man when Percy Cuthbert retired. It was a job which he enjoyed for several years until his own retirement.

He and I were treated as part of the Rileys' extended family – a strange and seemingly disparate group, but it really worked. I was supposed to be there as Mary's friend, but at sixteen and seventeen I was far more attracted to Mrs Riley and Mrs Turner than to the children, whom I tolerated and played with for the sake of the tremendous welcome and affection they all showed me and the difference in atmosphere between this family and my own circumscribed home life. The family friendship even extended occasionally to my parents when the Rileys were invited to our house for the evening. All the females played Monopoly and Mr Riley and my father played chess. These sessions often lasted until three or four in the morning, to my great pleasure, my mother's tacit acceptance, and my father's quiet enjoyment of another man's company.

I was always instructed to come home early from my evenings at Prospect Farm and, regardless of the instruction, I always returned shortly after eleven from an evening of relaxed play, convivial conversation and laughter and a delicious supper, to find my parents ready for bed, my mother with her hair in curlers, a little tight-lipped, leaning on the fireguard, my father impassively sitting in the rocking chair, waiting for my arrival. I resented the fact that, although I was sixteen, then seventeen, and they were perfectly happy for me to walk in the back lanes by myself during summer evenings, in no circumstances would they have gone to bed without supervising my return from a house a few hundred yards up the road and ensuring that I was first up the stairs and my father, as 'head of the household', could lock the back door. On one occasion I pointed out that they could go to bed and I could lock the door, but was promptly given to understand that such an arrangement would be totally unacceptable, whatever my age.

For months on end the war on the ground seemed quite remote: news now came from the Russian front, the Middle East, the Far East, including Burma. The war at sea continued and there were statistics of losses, but the ageing U-boat fleet was becoming less able to inflict damage and more convoys were crossing the Atlantic safely: between early April and mid-May fourteen of twenty-two convoys had crossed without loss and more than thirty U-boats had been sunk during the first two weeks of May.[20] RAF morale was boosted by the much publicized success of the 'Dambusters' raid on 16 May 1943, the appalling level of casualties among the air crews being regarded as inevitable and the limited achievement of their objectives being overplayed. Nearer home, the Free French, under Charles de Gaulle, were building an increasingly effective resistance and sabotage movement in France in preparation for the anticipated return to the continent of Allied forces, including Americans, referred to as the 'Second Front', the prospect of which seemed always to be in the near future, but not imminent.

One significant event did not make the news headlines. On 21 January the Casablanca Directive issued by the Combined Chiefs of Staff changed the strategic use of Bomber Command:

'Your primary objective will be the progressive destruction and dislocation of the German military, industrial and economic

---

[20] Entry for 19 May, 1943, *Chronology* 153.

system, and the undermining of the morale of the German people to a point where their capacity for armed resistance is fatally weakened.'

This directive led to the Battle of the Ruhr and round-the-clock bombing by the RAF and USAAF. Harris was officially free to pursue his preferred policy, namely, intensive bombing of German cities resulting in their devastation by a combination of high explosive and incendiary bombs. He calculated that this would be worth the high losses of planes and men and inevitable killing of civilian populations. It would significantly demoralize the enemy, and could shorten the war, even bring it to a successful conclusion, regardless of what the other armed forces might achieve on land or at sea.

In our otherwise quiet village, most evenings now ended with the sight and sound of the massed bombers from Leeming, Dishforth and Linton heading east. It was an intensification of the constant activity in the skies which for several years had provided the background drone that we tuned out as we went about our daily lives. At the time its significance was not obvious to us, in spite of regular news bulletins relaying a narrative of cities targeted, objectives achieved and losses incurred. Retrospectively it can be understood as the implementation of this new strategy by our local squadrons.

Though the campaign continued through that summer and the following winter, memories blur into one image of summer sunset and dark shapes, at once exciting, sobering and comforting, providing for us as observers a lifting of the heart and a feeling that something was being done to bring the war to the enemy. While it was happening we had no means of understanding the propaganda with which the nation was being fed or beginning to interpret the statistics in terms of human suffering. A visit to any of the museums and a study of the literature now available puts what seemed acceptable to a nation accustomed to life in wartime, to whom photographs of what was actually taking place were unavailable, into a horrifying context. Young men were forced to go night after night deep into enemy territory, knowing the likelihood that they would soon face the same fate as that of their comrades who had failed to return. Comparatively few crew members survived to earn their break after thirty missions, quite apart from the fact that they had no option but to pour their load of high explosive and incendiary devices into cities where civilians would be subjected to horrors which when compared to what had happened to London, Coventry, Southampton and other English cities were relatively insignificant, bad as it was if you were involved.

From the end of 1942 to April 1944 'Bomber' Harris supervised and extended an appallingly costly campaign to demolish Berlin, which lay at the limits of the planes' capability,[21] together with sustained attacks on other more accessible German cities, the main attack falling particularly on the industrial area of the Ruhr. The short campaign against Hamburg followed in July and early August, 1943. This caused a devastating firestorm because of a combination of weather conditions, and temporarily put that important city out of the war effort. What is regarded as 'the Battle of Berlin' took place between 23 August, 1943 and 24 March, 1944, and involved nineteen raids on the city. These raids represented slightly less than half of Bomber Command's effort during the period, and most were carried out by Lancasters, the planes now forming our local squadrons. During this period of mixed assaults we believed that we could tell from the direction of flight and next day's news which of the major cities they were heading for; this may have been the case to some extent because the strategy involved repeated visits to a number of targets.

Max Hastings has described how 76 squadron, one of Group 4's units of Halifaxes then based at Linton-on-Ouse, flew night after night to heavily defended targets. Throughout the Battle of the Ruhr the squadron steadily lost one, sometimes two aircraft a night. In 1943 they operated on 140 nights and lost 59 aircraft, three times their average operating strength.[22] The statistics of

[21] Martin Middlebrook, *The Berlin Raids: RAF Bomber Command, Winter 1943-4* (London: Penguin Books, 1990).

[22] Hastings, *Bomber Command*, 196-7.

the Berlin raids alone reveal the enormous cost of this changed policy in men and planes, not considering the destruction and loss of life on the ground. Two squadrons of Lancasters from Linton were involved: 426 Squadron dispatched 210 Lancaster sorties on eighteen Berlin raids, with 13 aircraft missing, three crashed and 88 men killed; 408 Squadron, consisting of mixed crews of mainly Canadians,[23] together with some English and American members, dispatched 205 sorties on fifteen raids, with 8 aircraft missing, 1 crashed and 57 men killed. These are just the statistics from one airfield in our local section of Group 4, Bomber Command. These high losses were a direct result of the distance over enemy territory that the planes were compelled to cover, working at the limits of their crews' endurance and open to the accurate fire-power of the German fighters and ground defences.

My memories of that summer are of the impressive numbers of planes regularly involved, making their contribution to that of their colleagues from bases situated down the whole of the east of the country. Among the more dramatic occasions must have been 23 May, 1943, the night of the raid on Dortmund, in which 754 bombers dropped 2,000 tons of bombs, or 12 June, when 693 bombers dropped close to the same number on Dusseldorf, or again, on 28 June, my mother's forty-eighth birthday, when more than 500 aircraft bombed Cologne. The general bombing campaign continued into the autumn, even intensifying as, for example, when on 22 September, over 650 aircraft dropped more than 2,300 bombs on Hanover. Of course, we had no access to such statistics at the time; news bulletins didn't give us the whole picture, just the names of places attacked and numbers of planes missing, as released by the armed forces to the Ministry of Information, processed by them and broadcast by the BBC. The reality could make no impact on the general public at the time, so

---

[23] The Canadians at Linton belonged to No.6 Group. During the 28 months of operations this group suffered one eighth of the total losses, killed or missing, borne by the whole of Bomber Command. Between the group's formation on 1 January, 1943, and VE-Day, 6,267 airmen were listed killed or missing. *Wings over Linton*, 102.

that doubts about the morality of what was happening did not dent our delusions about the validity of the campaign.

To us, these RAF crews were heroes helping to win the war. We didn't fully appreciate, either, the loss of young lives resulting from the prodigal use of highly trained men, many of them still in their teens, in pursuit of this dubious objective, to destroy enemy cities and demoralize their people. Perhaps it was just as well, because we could only accept it. My parents seemed undisturbed by moral questions, and as a teenager I certainly took everything at face value and interpreted what I saw romantically as portrayed in popular songs and the occasional cinema newsreel. One of my favourite *Picture Post* covers showed a Lancaster from one of the Linton squadrons outlined against the sky, a romantic photograph of a beautiful plane, dissociated from the broken images which we didn't see. Sometimes reality touched us. On one occasion Jack was standing chatting with us in the girls' yard as he frequently did before going home, watching the Lancasters rising from Linton to join the massed squadrons. He said sadly, 'We lost my plane last night.' Isla Moore, about three years older than me, and her husband, an air-crew member flying from Linton, lodged with Mr and Mrs Cooper across the road from the school. We used to see him cycling to work; then one night he didn't return and she was a widow at twenty.

At some point during that summer of 1943 a memorable incident occurred just as we were having tea. We became aware of an unusual sound from the engine of a light aircraft flying low, puttering and fading. It narrowly missed the roofs of the school and our house and we saw it cross the road in the gap between the cottages and come down with a violent explosion just beyond Parkers' garden. Foolishly, we dashed out to see what was happening, and there were pieces of debris – large and small pieces of light metal – floating in the air and crashing to the ground in the gardens, the street and Jackson's field. One of these floated over my head and I was merely excited, when I should have taken cover. It didn't have my name on it and landed safely in the field, and I picked up a trophy in the garden, a shapely piece of some very lightweight alloy. Over the next few days we saw teams of investigators combing the area, meticulously searching. Eventually I confessed to one of them that I had this piece and handed it over. He thanked me and said it was something they had particularly been looking for. It looked very ordinary to me; perhaps he wished to impress me with the importance of every scrap of debris in such an inquiry. We learned from Jack the story coming out of Linton, that the aircraft was carrying several VIPs from the armed forces who were to be involved in discussions with the Russians, and that it had been sabotaged. Of course there was no way of checking this and nothing reached the national news.

Our year in the Lower Sixth ended and the summer holiday was a welcome break. 'Holidays at home' were taken for granted, but this one was particularly memorable. Mr Riley cleaned out an old wooden barn in one of his remoter fields near the river, so that we could set up a camp. He carried down the heavier things on his tractor and trailer: a stove and paraffin, crockery, frying pan, saucepans and a kettle, washing-up bowl, boxes to sit on and use as tables, deck chairs and camp stools, a large container of water, the wind-up gramophone and records, ours and theirs, and a garden fork. Mary, Paula, Vincent Reed and I would gather peas from the Rileys' garden and carry them, together with slices of home-cured ham, bread, butter, tea, coffee and sugar in baskets on our bikes, all the way down Church Lane, through the gate at the bottom, down the rutted lane, across a couple of rough meadows, to the camp.

Then we set out our cooking gear and took the fork to the nearby potato field and dug sufficient new potatoes for however many people would be at lunch. Sometimes Mrs Riley and Mrs Turner walked down, sometimes my parents came on their bikes, sometimes there were just the four of us. Soon the peas would be shelled and the scraped new potatoes would be simmering, the aroma of sizzling ham would banish the lingering smell of hay and compacted earth, and we would set out our dining table, complete with cloth, on the inverted boxes. Making the meal was the main activity; it tasted as only really fresh produce can and we never wanted an alternative. When we had eaten and washed up we played the inevitable ball games or listened to records, such favourites as *Felix kept on walking* and a saucy record entitled *Down in the fields where the buttercups all grow*, which told the story of a youth and his girl who went there, despite the fact that, after the cows had been down there a bit, it was not a nice place for a lady to sit. Unfortunately, the young lady got a bee down her back, which her swain attempted to remove, only to receive a slap, though he claimed that he 'didn't know that bee was so far below'. Daring stuff, and we loved it!

It was a fine, dry summer and we went down to the camp whenever we could. Ken and Doris came to stay with us for a week and joined the party. At the end of the day it was a joy to cycle back as the sun was setting, feeling absolutely content, and we were very sorry to pack up the camp at the end of August and leave the barn empty. We were never able to repeat the experience. By the following summer the field had been ploughed, in accordance with wartime requirements for ever-increasing use of even marginal land to grow crops. That year the Rileys had two schoolboys, sixth-formers of my own age, staying with them to work on the farm, as many youngsters did in their summer holidays to make their contribution to the war effort. They were happy to join our evening games of cricket or play hide and seek in the farmyard and buildings.

In September, 1943, when the school holidays were over, my mother joined me on the bus. Her age group was now required to do work of national importance and she had returned gladly to teaching, being given a post at the Castle Yard School in Knaresborough. This she did for that school year before being allowed to teach in Great Ouseburn school. Mrs Walker had retired and her replacement was travelling from Knaresborough on the bus that was taking us in. When the illogicality of this was pointed out, the West Riding waived its rigid rule that no member of a head teacher's family could work in the same school, and the two women exchanged jobs. My mother had always resented being compelled to leave teaching on marriage, and she stayed at the village school until her own retirement, happy to return to the career she enjoyed.

Our final year at school began with the prospect of applying for places at university or college. The normal four-year university course for training graduate teachers had been condensed into three years because of the war, with additional short terms tucked into what would have been the summer vacations and only two terms to reach intermediate standard. Two years and a term would gain us a degree in our teaching subject and the last two terms would be for professional training.

Vera and I both applied for places at Leeds University to read English Language and Literature and, early in 1944, we went for interview. I can just remember the interview with the tutor of women students, Miss Hibgame, a lady of great dignity, with a greying bun and kindly, reassuring manner. But my outstanding memory is of riding up Woodhouse Lane in a tram, to where the new Parkinson building, with its impressive tower, complete but not yet open, was blocked off by a high wooden fence on which someone had painted in large, white letters: SPEED THE SECOND FRONT! BUT WE'RE RESERVED, MR BEVIN, WE'RE RESERVED! I thought to myself that this was the future, the anarchic life of a student in which you could paint slogans on hoardings and be really wild, and I longed to embrace the freedom it represented. Well, it turned out to be carefully regulated freedom, but we accepted that, since we, like many of those old enough to fight and die, were minors until the age of twenty-one. I was offered a place and looked forward to my new status with pride and some apprehension at the prospect of such a radical change to my life. All that stood between me and this exciting prospect was the need for as good a result in the Higher School Certificate examinations as had been predicted, and a lot of hard work to achieve it, particularly the obligatory Latin.

Our route to school took us to the end of Marton Lane and across the Great North Road (A1) to the Arkendale road, a couple of hundred yards further on, a simple manoeuvre on this single carriageway in most circumstances. One bright morning early in June there was a difference. We came to a stop at the lane end; the main road was full of an unbroken stream of military vehicles of all descriptions trundling south. From tanks to jeeps they formed a menacing display of power and we felt awed and emotional as our driver waited for a chance to cross the road, because we sensed that this was more than just routine troop deployment. A couple of days later, on 6 June, the news of the D-Day landings came over the wireless and we realized that what we had seen was just a fraction of the man-power on the move that day. We felt to have been involved because we had seen it, seen the faces of the men in battle dress moving sombrely towards their destiny. Those very men and vehicles had crossed the Channel and were now fighting in France. Some would already have died on the hazardous crossing and on the Normandy beach-heads.

On 13 June the Germans launched their first flying bomb attack on the south coast. These missiles were launched regularly over the next few weeks and terrified people living in the coastal towns because of their random unpredictability. We had our third group of evacuees, senior schoolchildren from Brighton. They were rough and tough compared with our rural youngsters and my dad used their surplus energy to good effect by ensuring that, along with his own senior pupils, the boys did a lot of heavy digging and the girls helped to clear the rubbish on the neglected patch he had taken over in the Oddfellows' allotments behind Burrell's yard and the back lane. Once again they stayed only a short time, because the main spate of rocket attacks didn't last long, and all evacuees felt the pull of home and their familiar lives. Comparative safety in a sleepy Yorkshire village can have had little appeal compared with being with their families in a working seaside town, even with the fear of 'doodlebugs'.

Uncle John and Auntie Jane, who then lived in Bognor Regis, were apprehensive about the missile attacks and asked if they could come and stay with us for a while. They remained for eight weeks, a trial for all of us, particularly as part of their visit intruded into the summer holidays and my preparations for university. I disliked Auntie Jane's attenuated baking days, when my mother and I came home to the delicious smell of cakes, pies and scones, unfortunately accompanied by a floury mess in the kitchen, but she wanted to pull her weight because my mother was working. She did pretty well considering her unfamiliarity with the paraffin stove and its movable oven, still in use. When electricity was installed in 1936, the West Riding, with characteristic parsimony where staff housing was concerned, had refused to sanction a cooker point in the kitchen on the grounds that there was a fire oven already in the living room range, despite my father's protest that it hadn't worked for years. We had an electric iron by then and no longer had to heat the old flat irons on the fire, but Jane's ironing sessions could trail on for hours, until she was satisfied that everything had been done to perfection, even the gussets in the tails of Uncle John's shirts. Whatever the day, we would come back on the bus to a job not quite done, with the meal to prepare and ingredients for school dinners to be weighed and potatoes to be boiled for the poultry.

At least, for me, the exams were over. Although we were still expected to be in school until the end of the summer term and had our duties as prefects, life during those last few weeks was one long pleasurable round of tennis, sitting in the sun with the staff, who were equally glad to relax, playing table tennis in the form room, and spending extended lunch hours in the Castle grounds or on the river.

One event involving the whole town took place during that term. From time to time there had been morale-boosting and money-raising national events. This one was *Wings for Victory Week*, and the guest of honour at the main celebration in the Castle yard was a distinguished local fighter pilot, called Lacey, who had won medals for outstanding service. He was a former pupil of King James's Grammar School who had been in the sixth form when I first went there. There had been a 'competition' for two sixth formers, a boy and a girl, to write an appropriate speech to be delivered from the platform on behalf of the school. Deryck Duncalf and Pauline Topham, both from Knaresborough, had been invited to enter and anyone else who wished to do so could take part. Nobody apart from me took up the offer. All three of us delivered our speeches from the stage in front of Mr Robinson and Miss Sawdon. They told me that my speech and delivery were undoubtedly the best, but that the boy and girl who spoke from the platform must be pupils who lived in Knaresborough. As a reward I was to present the visitor with a silver cigarette case when he addressed the school. I felt the unfairness of this, but naively hadn't realized that there was no competition. Deryck and Pauline spoke well, but I would have loved to have been up there performing. One thing I did during those last few weeks was to organize a magazine, which we called *The Prefectorial*, containing poetry, humour, news, and a satirical association of members of staff with popular song titles. When I had twisted a few arms for contributions and provided some myself, I wrote it out on my father's 'cyclostyle', an old-fashioned, manually operated duplicator, and printed off as many copies as I could beg paper for, and we sold it in school to raise money for the 'Wings for Victory' campaign. I still have a rather faint copy in my old desk.

It was no easier at home when term ended. I was annoyed by Uncle John's persistent supervision of my every activity, even to telling me how he expected to have his bread buttered, that is, with the butter spread thinly and evenly right to the edge of the crust, like putting on a professional coat of paint. There were no arguments, because we had to get along together; he and I went for walks and collected bunches of wild flowers and, having once been a member of a choral society, he tried to advise me on how to sing. I didn't take the message on board, but enjoyed the serious attention because, much as I loved singing, my parents had never allowed me to have lessons from Mrs Marshall, who had been my piano teacher when I was younger. Auntie Jane, as ever, was ponderously slow and pleasant. It was a relief to us all when they went back home. They bought me a green-handled toasting fork as my going-to-university present. I called it Mephistopheles because we had recently read Marlowe's *Dr Faustus*. Over the next four years it toasted endless slices of bread at the small electric fire in my room where I cooked scrambled dried egg, and it served well over the next thirty or so while we still had open fires, gradually losing its green paint. Shortly afterwards, John and Jane moved to Camberley to be near Madge and Lew again, and that was where we visited them when the war was over.

189

With our family routine restored, we prepared for my departure to Leeds. I had very few clothes apart from school uniform, but my mother was generous with her clothing coupons and we were able to buy new underwear and enough new material to make a winter coat and a smart dress for informal dances. Two new skirts were made by unpicking my mother's old ones and cutting panels from the pieces. As we had been doing throughout the war, we unpicked old, hand-knitted jumpers with usable wool, washed the wool in hanks to straighten it, and made new jumpers, either short sleeved or in a lacy pattern. I was bridesmaid to Miss Dawson when she married Bill Flatman that summer, which meant that I had a full-length dress in an unusual autumn leaf colour that my mother made for that occasion, which would serve for formal wear. There was blackout material left over after making our own and the school curtains and we used some of this to make an elegant, full-length dressing gown. We bought brightly coloured 'ric-rac' braid to decorate it, back and front, with a dragon-like pattern. It was heavy to wear and had a strange, persistent chemical smell when warm, but I loved the fine texture and sheen of this black fabric. It fitted beautifully and I enjoyed it for many years.

PART 3
BEYOND THE VALE

Chapter XIII

University Life in Wartime

The last year of the war saw me adapting to life in the English Department at Leeds University, provisionally as an honours student. During the first week of October, 1944 the small petrol ration was used to take me and my suitcase to Oxley Hall, one of the two university hostels for women students in Far Headingley, where, for the first time in my life, I would be free to make my own decisions from day to day, responsible only to myself for making friendships and working to retain my privileged university place. I welcomed it and it terrified me, not least because of the shortened course and the pressure of new subjects, particularly Anglo-Saxon, a completely new language, with its accompanying course in phonology, the history of linguistic change. Fortunately, the university decided that the international situation was sufficiently promising for the course to be lengthened to the original four years, and we found to our relief that we had the full three terms before the intermediate exams, with the subsequent assessment of whether our position in the honours school would be confirmed.

As a nominal condition of our exemption from service in the armed forces, we were to undertake 'work of national importance' outside the university for one evening a week. Some people worked in canteens; one of my friends spent her evening helping in St George's Crypt, a shelter for homeless men in a church behind Leeds Town Hall, which provided a meal and a bed for the night. I went to lead a drama group at a youth club in Osmondthorpe, one of the poorer, working-class areas of Leeds. The fourteen-year-olds were pleasant youngsters and we enjoyed ourselves; I felt I had an easy option. The club leader was friendly, but had a firm hand on the general organization of activities and expected good behaviour. In contrast to city life today, I felt absolutely safe alone in that area in the dark autumn and winter evenings, as I walked to and from the youth club, waited for the tram to take me to the city centre and waited again for another out to Far Headingley.

During that last year of the war I missed two events in the village. The first was the crash of a fully laden bomber from Linton. Failing to take off successfully, it landed in a stand of beech trees just across the road from Little Ouseburn church. The blast from the impact of the plane and explosion of its bomb load severely damaged the Meysey-Thompson mausoleum, a prominent feature of the churchyard, shifted the ancient, square church tower marginally on its foundation and damaged the glass. A few windows in the school and nearby houses were broken, but the feeling was that the impact of the blast on the church and mausoleum had helped to save the village from further damage. The stand of trees, which originally had an elegant outline, is still mis-shapen, a lasting memorial to the crew who were killed. Apparently take-off with a full load was always a vulnerable time in the operation, particularly when the plane was expected to carry a heavier weight than originally intended.

The second, almost non-event, was the strafing of the village with machine-gun fire by a rogue German fighter plane as it tried to make its way home. Nobody was hurt, because nobody was out on the street, but some minor damage was done; one bullet chipped a stone in the school house near the back door, so no doubt the house still bears its mark from wartime action.

From my point of view, the war receded into the background. As students we rarely listened to the wireless; we were far too busy enjoying our social life and working under some stress to reach a standard which we hoped would be sufficiently good, but couldn't be sure of until tested and assessed. There were just twenty of us in the provisional English Honours class in the first year, including one man, unattractive to the women in spite of his broad smile, a trombonist in the

Salvation Army, permanently and satirically referred to as *Mr Peel*, with a mocking intonation; I never knew his Christian name.

Life in Oxley Hall was well regulated under the gracious supervision of the warden, Miss Maclaren, a well made but elegant, grey-haired, handsome woman, who made a point of knowing all the students personally and having her ear to the ground on what was happening in hall. To make sure that she knew everyone, she invited small groups of students for pre-dinner, non-alcoholic cocktails with an unspeakably exotic flavour, and strangely seasoned small savouries, in her beautifully furnished sitting room which was   strategically placed near the front entrance to the old house. Dinner, a two-course meal with delicious puddings, served at seven thirty, was always relatively formal, in that we gathered in the common room and awaited Miss Maclaren and the group who were joining her at the high table that evening. A regular visitor was the Roman Catholic Bishop of Leeds, a near neighbour. When she led the way across to the dining room we filed in after her. High table was a trial unless you were one of the experienced senior students, but no doubt good for our social education. On my first occasion I was sitting next to the warden; while painfully making conversation and being extra careful of my table manners, I managed to shoot a pea onto her plate. I was inclined to blush easily at any time!

Ordinarily, we tried to avoid sitting at the table headed by the sub-warden, Miss Boynes, a lecturer in law and a humourless, condescending conversationalist with a deep, portentous voice. Miss Maclaren and Miss Boynes always wore full length, formal dresses, Miss Maclaren usually in blue, decorative and lacy, with heavy jewellery, Miss Boynes in brown, simply cut. At the end of the meal we stood until the group from high table, joined by Miss Boynes, had walked out down the full length of the dining room; then we were able to relax and chat as we followed.

We were exceptionally well fed. Breakfast was bacon or sausage, with fried bread, mushrooms and tomato, or scrambled egg on toast, or a kipper, always with ample toast and marmalade. We had a hostel ticket which entitled us to a two-course lunch in the university refectory; snacks and drinks of tea, coffee and 'national milk cocoa', a thick, sweet, drinking chocolate made from a powdered mix, were always available in the union cafeteria; we had 'coffins' in the corridor outside our rooms at Oxley in which we kept our own crockery, cutlery and a pan, and part of our tea, coffee, margarine, jam and sugar ration and any extras we bought, so that we could make afternoon tea when we came in from lectures and at the weekends. Our only source of heat in the room was a small electric fire which we tipped onto its back to cook the notorious scrambled dried egg. This was relished by most of my friends, who didn't have poultry at home. Bread was always available from the kitchen and toast was made by holding the bread as close as possible to the elements. There were electric kettles in the 'stu-pan', the kitchenette at the end of each corridor, attached to which was a drying room for our washing, dabbled inadequately in the sink. Even after dinner it was not unknown for us to make a supper snack with our last hot drink. We put on weight.

As the warden of the hostel was officially *in loco parentis* to us as minors, our whereabouts in the evenings had to be known to her. During the first year our access to social events in the University Students' Union and cinema or theatre visits in town, was restricted to two late evenings a week. We signed out of the hostel, and dinner if necessary, saying which event we were attending, and were expected to be back in Oxley routinely by eleven o'clock, later at the weekends or if the event necessitated it. More flexibility was allowed as we gained seniority. Special permission was needed to attend formal union balls, which ended later, but it was always granted. These restrictions were acceptable to us, as we knew that everyone would need to be accounted for in an emergency and, in practice, we could do as much as we wished in the union or in town, our available time and money being limited. The trams stopped running before midnight and the last few only went as far as the Headingley depot at the end of Weetwood Lane and, in any case, we sometimes preferred to walk back. More than one hasty goodnight was said to a conscientious escort as he hurried to catch the last tram back towards town. Often a group of girls who had gone together returned together. The blackout didn't worry us; Bryan's fish and chip shop was open on the corner, and a short walk up the lane eating our two-pennyworth of chips with 'scraps' of batter, or even a portion of fish with them if we were willing to spend eightpence, made a convivial end to the evening.

Union functions and society meetings were at the centre of the wider student life. There were only around seventeen hundred students in the whole university, including the medical and dental schools. The central venue for Saturday dances, society balls, drama productions and official union meetings was the Riley Smith Hall, which could contain the whole student body when necessary. The AGM to elect union officials was a riotous occasion, with toilet roll streamers and flour-bag bombs and much barracking of the union officials and candidates for office who occupied the platform. Exciting rumours floated round the union from time to time, such as that of the 'de-bagging', yet again, of some unpopular member, whose trousers would be hoisted high in a convenient public position. We knew by sight the most prominent or notorious students and derived vicarious pleasure from such proximity.

There were separate men's and women's common rooms, where one could sit and chat, or read quietly, and a larger room where society meetings and lunchtime hops and concerts were held, but the most popular venues were the cafeteria and the Joint Common Room. The cafeteria had a balcony, still preserved, but subsumed in later additions. In the 1940s it was in the open air, looking down on old Victorian terraces, already owned by the university and scheduled for demolition to make way for the ambitious projected post-war building plan, which eventually became a glass and concrete reality in the fifties and sixties. On fine days we took our cocoa and biscuits out there. Symbolically, we felt to be towering over these cramped streets, with shabbily dressed women sitting out on the doorsteps in fine weather, chatting or minding young children. It made us very aware of our privileged position and total insulation from life in the inner city. My friend, Eileen, came from a strongly socialist family in Stoke-on-Trent and would philosophize about these matters, but I'm ashamed to say it reinforced the sense of being different and superior that my village upbringing had engendered.

197

The Joint Common Room was the comfortable social centre, with groups of leather sofas and easy chairs in which to relax and chat, or meet friends of both sexes from different departments between lectures and in the lunch hour and find out about society meetings, all of which were advertised on hand-written posters on the walls. Rag Day, in the summer, was a major union money-raising event for charity, in which most students took part. We dressed and made up our faces as eccentrically as possible and went around the town shaking tins and selling copies of *The Gryphon,* the union magazine. The public responded generously and with good humour.

There was an excellent common room in Oxley Hall, with a beautifully polished wooden floor, an ideal venue for attractive social events nearer than the union or the city centre. We had entertainment every weekend: people put on plays and I was able to indulge my love of acting; there were students who could play the piano or sing well; routinely, we had a Saturday night hop, when we danced to records, and every term there was a formal dance to which we could invite a male partner, and there was no shortage of men willing to accept the invitation. There was even a 'sitting out room' on these occasions, opposite Miss Maclaren's sitting room, of course. It was dimly and atmospherically lit – communal, but we didn't notice anyone else. We could entertain men in our rooms until nine o'clock on these occasions, whereas the time limit for male visitors on any other day was six o'clock, and no questions were asked about how often our visitors came.

Occasionally the men from Devonshire Hall would 'raid' us, usually egged on by their women friends, who would conveniently open ground-floor windows. This drove Miss Boynes frantic. She would storm down the ground-floor corridor of the new wing, where her room was situated, lamenting in her booming contralto voice that there were 'men in hall', oblivious to the fact that there might be one hiding under the bed of the student representative deputed to check, who had been forewarned by the sound of her approach. On one such occasion an adventurous visitor hung a pair of braces on her door; they remained undiscovered long enough to entertain the appreciative ground-floor students and others who heard about it on the grapevine and tiptoed along to view this aberration with its incongruously salacious implications. Oh yes, the student experience!

Traditionally, as Christmas approached, Oxley students who enjoyed singing formed a choir to learn carols. Some of these were beautiful and unusual arrangements and we learned the soprano and alto parts. The Devon men had a similar choir, learning the tenor and bass parts, and one evening, near the end of term, the two choirs performed in the spectacular entrance hall of the old house, the original Oxley Hall onto which the extension had been built when it was bought for conversion into a hostel. The spectators sat on the impressive, curved staircase and round the balcony. Coffee and home-made mince pies were available afterwards in the dining room.

On the evening of Shrove Tuesday the cook provided a large bowl of batter and extra sugar for members of the SCM (Student Christian Movement) who had elected to make pancakes in their rooms and sell them to raise money for an appropriate charity. Despite the lateness of the hour and the previous dinner there were few abstainers from this supper treat.

We were allowed three weekends a term at home, but we didn't always take them because there was so much to do in town or at the union or out walking with friends on the days when we had no lectures. Traditionally we cleaned our rooms on Saturday mornings when a change of bed linen was brought round, but that wasn't necessarily a serious chore. On Sundays people who were accustomed to doing so attended their preferred church, including Jackie, a Methodist and Joan, a Baptist, but Eileen and I quite often went for a walk in the open country, along the Ring Road to the corner by the Moortown water tower, or round Adel village. Another favourite walk was through The Hollies, a park with a few formal beds near the entrance, and attractive woodland which led down a steep slope to Meanwood Beck and a stream-side path. At the weekends, too, we always had communal afternoon tea in our 'families', the name given in the hostels to the friendship groups of people who shared rooms or interests. Everybody joined a 'family' and I have remained in touch with the three closest members of mine throughout life.

Our family consisted originally of six people, two reading English, one reading French, two biologists and one chemist. Only Ida, the chemist, was not a Recognized Student in Training, and she left on completing her degree. Heather, with whom the rest of us had less in common, drifted away.

Whenever I went home for the weekend my parents smothered me with questions. My mother would have made a fruit cake for me to take back; they were generous with pocket money and would have given me as much as I could claim to need, but I wouldn't accept more than five pounds in small change. I enjoyed the challenge of being economical, probably as a result of living so long with wartime restrictions, and always made it last until the next visit. Most of my friends were conscious that it was a sacrifice on their parents' part to allow them the opportunity to go to university. They had very little to spend, so they took pride in never spending a penny more than necessary, a point of view which I shared as a matter of principle, though both my parents were working and I was an only child. I had always taken it for granted that the money would be available for me to go into some form of higher education, but even so I wasted nothing.

My main problem was of a different order and not shared by the others. It seemed very strange, even during my first year as a student, to return to the village after this differently regulated life of responsible independence. My parents still regarded me as the child I had been. As I was soon to discover, the others all went home to relaxed, affectionate, demonstrative families. In Eileen's home, for example, when I went to spend a weekend or part of our vacations with her, I found the same easy-going, welcoming reception that characterized the Rileys and a warm-hearted informal comradeship between family members: Mrs Walker was chatty and a delight, treated me as another family member; Mr Walker, always a man of few words in this family of articulate women, smiled warmly at me and made me feel welcome, and Eileen's younger sister, Doreen, was lively and entertaining. Chris Shaw, a close friend who was a day student in the English department, sometimes invited me home on Saturday afternoons, or even to stay overnight. She was a vicar's daughter with three

200

sisters. They and their mother, a former domestic science teacher and excellent cook, laughed and joked and enjoyed cosy domesticity, knitting or sewing round the fireside, while father sat amiably in the corner of the large vicarage kitchen, occasionally joining in, but usually reading.

My mother, in contrast, expected me to give her an account of my university life and friendships, ask her permission and seek my father's agreement if I wanted to go out to the Rileys or to York on the bus, with the same serious-faced, inquisitional control she had always enjoyed. During the four years I was at the university they became a little more accustomed to the fact that I made my own decisions, but, in the areas where it mattered, neither of my parents recognized my need for independence. I knew, also, that they would have been embarrassingly formal and ill at ease if I had invited friends to stay, because they couldn't relax and be natural with outsiders. As a result, increasingly, I spent a large part of my vacations elsewhere, so that they complained plaintively that they hardly ever saw me.

Over my four years at university I relished new holiday experiences in the vacations such as youth hostelling, in Wales with Eileen and Doreen, on Skye with Chris, Josie and Nancy; escaped from the claustrophobic surroundings where I felt constrained by obligation and solemn duty; fled from the intuitive knowledge that my parents' life together had been centred on their emotional investment in me; but I couldn't escape the guilt I felt over my firm intention to resist their expectation that I would ultimately work in the locality and live at home. Their determined and brittle cheerfulness in the face of the inevitable became particularly uncomfortable when, as a graduate in my fourth year, I brought home the dear friend with whom I had shared many teas of scrambled dried egg on toast and 'conversation' in the absence of my understanding room-mate.

Even before the end of that first year all these dissonances and potential conflicts of outlook and expectation had become apparent to me; away from home I was acquiring standards of comparison which made it clear that the homes of my school friends, with whom I had stayed occasionally by hard-won permission of my parents, had represented the norm, and my horizons widened.

With the summer term of 1945 came the certainty that the war in Europe would soon end, as the Allied armies swept across Germany. On 13 April, 1945 Belsen and Buchenwald had been liberated and the full horrors of the Nazi extermination camps began to emerge. On 19 April Richard Dimbleby, who went into Belsen with the British forces, reported from the concentration camp an eye-witness description of the living skeletons incarcerated there.[24] The full inhumanity of the Nazi regime was exposed to the outside world and the reports shocked the nation, even more so as photographs began to appear in newspapers and on cinema newsreels. Our main pictorial impression of the war came from these newsreels; we were accustomed to dramatic films of battles in progress, on land or in the air. There was a news cinema in Leeds city centre, as well as newsreels accompanying films at the other cinemas. When pressure of work and too much company made me long to escape, I used to go into town and take refuge in the cinema, gazing at the screen through the haze of swirling tobacco smoke. Usually it had the same function as the library box in the village schoolroom, but these pictures were of a different order; nothing like them had ever been seen before.

The announcement of the end of hostilities was known to be imminent and on 8 May, 1945 we heard that the war in Europe had ended, bringing relief mixed with a certain sense of anti-climax. I didn't go home for the official V. E. Day celebrations but Deryck Duncalf, the school friend who was studying medicine and with whom I had occasionally gone out during our first year at Leeds, went home to Knaresborough to attend the town's festivities with his family. There was a dance in the Riley Smith Hall on the Saturday evening and most

---

[24] Barnard, *We interrupt this programme:* 51.

people remaining in Oxley that weekend went down to celebrate.

Term was not quite over and the end-of-year results were imminent. When the lists were posted we went down to the University and scanned them apprehensively. The individual English papers were not graded in order of merit, but I was delighted to learn that I had qualified for the honours course and was entitled to proceed with my proposed degree in English Language and Literature with subsidiary History. To my amazement I had come second on the year list in the History course I had taken. There were seventy or more candidates because some courses were run every other year and taken by any student, including honours students, whose degree contained a history component. Professor Le Patourel's course on Mediaeval Life and Thought had been one of those revelations that change one's outlook; I realized for the first time that history can be an exciting human story of the activities and mentalities of ordinary people, and was hooked as a potential social historian after hearing his first lecture. The first-year examinations aimed to select those who could be expected to achieve at least a second class honours in finals; usually only one first was awarded in most arts departments, perhaps two if there were exceptional candidates; thirds were for the few who didn't fulfil expectations. Two members of our 'family' didn't attain the necessary qualifying standard in their honours subject and moved to a less specialized pass-degree course.

During the summer vacation, on 26 July, we heard of the Allies' ultimatum to Japan and, on 6 August, news bulletins announced the successful making of an atomic bomb by British scientists. On 9 August it was announced that one such bomb had been dropped on Hiroshima; the nation was shocked by descriptions and pictures of its devastating effects, but did not then understand their implications. The second, on Nagasaki, followed, and on 14 August, when we were visiting Uncle John and Auntie Jane in Camberley, Japan surrendered. V. J. Day was announced on 15 August, but did not have the same impact on us as the victory in Europe, which marked the end of the direct threat to our own future as a nation. The war was finally over, but the controversy over the dropping of the bomb was only just beginning, as some of its wider implications and after-effects became known.

CHAPTER XIV

The aftermath

In October, 1945 we returned to Leeds University for our second year. Our smaller honours group reading English had already met some of the staff in the School of English during our first year, men who had not joined the armed forces. Among them was Wilfred Roland Childe, benevolent in disposition and a true eccentric. The story was that he had come out of retirement for the duration of the war, and we accepted this as credible because he seemed so old. I discovered later that he was a long-established member of the Department of English Literature, but only in his late fifties when we knew him. A bachelor and devout Roman Catholic, he was a respected minor poet of the twenties and thirties, writing emotional poems, mostly on religious themes. He was a noticeable figure around the university, with his domed, bald pate fringed by fine, straggly hair, and thin, full-lipped, red-cheeked face. All the staff wore gowns, many of them well used, but Mr Childe's hung in shreds about his tall, angular body, moving to its own independent rhythm, held together round his shoulders by its yoke. His lectures on the poetic image, delivered in a monotone at incredible speed, were incomprehensible to us, and many of us soon decided that we preferred to work in the library rather than waste the hour.

His tutorials were a different matter. Tutorial groups consisted of five or six students and I was in his group. Each week one member read a paper on some aspect of our course to stimulate group discussion; in this case the theme was the Romantic poets. We sat in a semi-circle in front of the desk in his study to listen, while Mr Childe, a kindly expression on his face and a pad of blank paper in front of him, would jot down occasional notes. Most of his attention appeared to be devoted to the careful drawing in ink of stained-glass-window saints with haloes and angels with wings. As the essay progressed, these would achieve fascinating beauty and complexity and attracted more of our attention than the ideas we were supposed to be evaluating. When the reading was complete, he would look up, smile, and say courteously, 'Thank you, Miss (surname); that was very nicely done.' The victim of the day would relax and feel gratified by the praise. Then he would pause, look directly at the reader: 'When you said that Shelley… what *exactly* did you mean? Do you think, perhaps…?' and we would realize the extent of his concentration on our argument and shrewd assessment of its weaknesses. Several tutorial notebooks dating from the 1940s and recording his formal assessment of individual students for the head of department remain among his memorabilia and books of published poetry in the Brotherton Library's Special Collections – fortunately not those involving our group.

As the academic year progressed there were changes in the department, particularly the return of Professor Bonamy Dobrée, who had been Professor of English Literature before serving in the army during the war. He was every inch the high-ranking English army officer, dapper, with well groomed grey hair, military bearing, slightly out-turned feet designed for marching, brisk manner and upper class accent. He had an incisive mind and was a clear and precise lecturer on eighteenth-century English Literature; we appreciated his carefully structured delivery. He was writing a definitive study of Swift's satire and by the end of the course we felt over-exposed to some of its least pleasant aspects. He led his tutorials, as he delivered his lectures, with ideas sparking in all directions, but impersonally, as if he were addressing the troops. His study, with shelves of beautifully bound books among the more functional volumes, reflected his taste as a member of the minor aristocracy, to which his family belonged. A high shelf was decorated with antique spirit barrels, and an aroma of spirits and good tobacco seemed to precede or follow him wherever he went, or so we would maintain; we used to joke that we'd better not strike a match in the tutorial when he was there, particularly after lunch. He radiated a general bonhomie which never reached his eyes; we felt that he didn't care to remember our names, as we were not among the privileged few who had his attention. One artistic student of shrewd perception and satirical turn of mind drew an incisive cartoon for *The Gryphon* showing him smiling and holding out his hand in greeting, saying, 'Call me Bonamy!'

We soon began to understand what his cosy pre-war English Literature Department had been like, as we were gradually joined on the course by ex-service men in their late twenties. Two of these were returning to finish degree courses they had begun before the war and one, in particular, who had been a captain in the army, had belonged to the small group of protégés whom Dobree had admitted to his social circle when, in an even smaller department, he and his wife had entertained promising students at home. This familiarity was not extended to the post-war generation, who were of a different social class. The other returning student, a specialist in English Language, was a brilliant scholar and went on to become a distinguished academic. There were several more, including one ordained from the College of the Resurrection in Mirfield, who was living in the ornate Hostel of the Resurrection in Springfield Mount. Doug Taylor, another returning student, an enormous man, inscrutable and silent, waited until we had left the university to invite my friend Chris to marry him, which she did, after much hesitation.

These men made us feel very young and naive, with their experience of life, capacity for mature analysis, fluency and skill in discussion and, above all, their confidence. Other ex-service men and women joined the first year and became prominent members of the English Society, to which we all belonged. From being a group of women aged just over nineteen, with one isolated male member, we became a mixed group. Awed by the newcomers, who gave the impression of being much more sophisticated than we were, we worked as hard as before, but with less conviction of our talent. Nevertheless, the second year examinations were completed successfully by the whole group and once again we were on vacation, only too aware that, in the following academic year, we would have the pressure of finals.

There was to be one last, unexpected consequence of the end of wartime restrictions. When we returned in October, 1946, we found several overseas students in the department, including a Dutch man and woman and a Norwegian, Georg Roppen. He was a post-graduate student from the University of Oslo, with immaculate spoken English, in Leeds to complete a thesis on the works of Samuel Butler. He became friendly with me and my two day-student friends in the English Department, Chris and Phyl, with whom I usually spent my working days. I soon slipped into the habit of sitting by Georg in the library, because I was tired of talking about work and looking anxiously at what the other two were studying. It was refreshing to be alongside someone doing something completely different, and he was good company. The four of us used to go to the refectory at lunch time.

During registration Georg had met a young day student from Mirfield who was enrolling in the Geography Department. He had other friends, students from his old school, and a group of us used to meet for lunch in the refectory. To cut a long story short, the winter that followed, 1946-7, was extremely harsh, with heavy snowfalls. The pavements were ice-packed for weeks. Chris, Phyl and I, along with Georg and Geoffrey, arranged to go youth hostelling in the Yorkshire Dales during the Easter vacation, by which time we expected the snow to have melted. Georg had been in a concentration camp during the war and his weakened constitution couldn't adapt to the unfamiliar, damp cold of a prolonged English winter, so different from the crisp, dry snow of his home village in northern Norway. He returned home prematurely, having suffered from pneumonia. We three girls and one tenacious man went youth hostelling, quite a tough, cold undertaking with the remnants of the snow still in drifts on the higher ground. Georg never came back, but Geoff and I have been together ever since.

As the months passed, the horrors of what had been lost on both sides throughout the war became obvious, and news bulletins lost the gloss of victory. In the university, as in everyday life, there was no neat ending separating war and peace: the academic discipline and social interludes continued until finals were successfully completed and I returned for my year of professional training. Male undergraduates who, like Geoff, had been too young to serve in the war, could elect to defer their compulsory national service in the armed forces until they had finished their university course, but they must complete it before embarking on their career. This had been his choice, with the result that we reluctantly postponed our marriage until this commitment was fulfilled, particularly since the period of service was extended from eighteen months to two years shortly after he began his basic training in Brecon. Fortunately, having completed this and officer training at Eaton Hall near Chester, he was not drafted to Korea when that war broke out in 1950, but sent to Preston and, later, to Liverpool. There he was promoted to the rank of acting captain with a local supervisory role in the Army Education Corps, a rare achievement during national service, where such rank could not be confirmed, and one which would certainly have led to a rewarding career in the regular army; but neither of us wanted him to join the army, with no choice of where he would be stationed and no settled home life. His next move would have almost certainly been abroad and we wanted stability and a home of our own after nearly six years of waiting.

Rationing and shortages continued. We were married in Little Ouseburn church on 21 June, 1952, two days after Geoff's discharge from the army, and when we went to live in 39 Albemarle Road, York in September we still had ration books and registered for basic groceries at a local shop. Throughout the six years we lived there the coal ration was inadequate to keep the house warm and we supplemented the allowance with unrationed briquettes, inefficient nuggets fashioned from coal dust and cement, judging by their reluctance to burn and the copious grey residue left behind. In such ways, uncomfortable rather than threatening, the consequences of the war rumbled on. Despite these inconveniences, to which as young adults we were accustomed by the experience of our teenage years, we were happy to begin our life together without the tensions of living in a country at war.

When the fighting ceased, though, I still had three more years ahead as a student. If I look for a symbol that epitomizes our new freedom to enjoy the long-awaited security of peacetime, one image recurs, visual and atmospheric, a composite memory, a mood painting rather than a single occasion: I am returning to Oxley Hall on foot with a companion or companions, leaving the Union after one of the Saturday evening dances during the post-war years. As we pass through Far Headingley around midnight, the street lights go off in sequence behind us and we walk on in the joy of our companionship and laughter, confident that life now is full of bright prospects and the future, whatever it may hold, no long threatens to tear apart the fabric of our daily lives; it is for living.

In Retrospect

In the introduction I speculated that Part II would be a learning process and it has been that and more. When I began to write down my wartime memories I did not fully realize the military significance of the area in which I had been living. During the late 1930s aerial activity had become the familiar background to daily life and wartime brought an added dimension since more small local airfields had been built. I was marginally aware of changes, saw new types of aircraft, noticed with excitement the periods of intense aerial activity, listened avidly to news of where raids had taken place and naïvely associated myself with the action because of what I had seen.

I was a child going into my teens when it all began and a university student when it ended, going through all the changes and personal anxieties of adolescence before 'teenagers' became a self-conscious group. We accepted our status as minors, legally considered too immature to vote, though old enough to work after fourteen and register for service in the armed forces before we were eighteen and fight and die for our country, though women did not serve on the front line. I cannot imagine what it must have been like for those of our number who trained as air crew in the bombers, or as fighter pilots, and had to come to terms with the immediate prospect of death, any night, sooner rather than later, and with the task of bringing death and destruction to others. At the time I did not think about it, and the gradual realization of the reality underlying what I saw and heard has been an emotional and thought-provoking experience.

The need to know more than I knew at the time about the role of Bomber Command during the war has led me to read first-hand accounts of these men's experiences at local airfields, at Linton-on-Ouse in particular, and in Yorkshire generally, and has taken me to the Bomber Command Museum at Elvington and the National War Museum at Duxford. The visit to Elvington was particularly poignant because it showed the maintenance work of local ground staff such as Jack Lovegrove, and contained photographs and brief personal details of crews from our local bases who worked and died together, and letters from individual airmen. That was where I saw the first photograph of the damage to Hanover taken from one of the bombers on the night of the attack and enlarged to feature prominently on a wall. This shocked me in spite of the sense of outrage previously evoked by the postcards I bought in Dresden in 2004 which first made me visualize the reality behind contemporary news bulletins and statistics which I thoughtlessly accepted at the time and had rarely reconsidered.

At Elvington I saw a reconstruction of one particularly famous Halifax bomber, *Friday the Thirteenth*, but this seemed a mere museum piece compared with the Lancaster at Duxford. I was standing looking at it and remembering that these became the most familiar planes in our skies, so deadly, vulnerable and fragile, when a man in his thirties, his wife and two sons of about seven and nine came and stood beside me. I turned to him and said, 'I used to watch those things flying over every night to bomb Germany.' He looked at me with something like awe, as if it were a new thought to him that anyone remained alive who had seen this, and we had a short conversation about where I had been living and what I could remember. I hope it made their sight of the Lancaster more meaningful.

I then moved round to where I could see the gun turret, visualizing the rear gunner in his lonely station, isolated from the rest of the crew, with views of the sky all around and barely room to stow his parachute, knowing that he was the man who could strike the attacker first and save the plane and his comrades, but also the first target for the enemy who might come upon him unseen. I thought about the first-hand accounts I'd read of grim returning flights with enemy fighters and anti-aircraft fire all around and hazardous journeys nursing damaged planes back to base. The facile emotions of popular, romantic, morale-boosting wartime songs echoed ironically through my mind: 'Silver wings in the moonlight' ... 'Coming in on a wing and a prayer'. When I was in my teens these words could move me to heights of easy emotion and thoughtless patriotism as I stood and watched the squadrons. In the sombre context of a war museum I just wanted to weep for the sheer weight of suffering caused by war with its dehumanizing of political issues, for the waste of promising lives, and the stress experienced by men who had been very little older than me, a few the same age in the end, flying in these planes to bring destruction to civilians and military targets alike on a scale far beyond anything known in our towns and cities, even though that was devastating to those who went through it:

'Well, sir, that was my thirtieth op, and I'm twenty-one tomorrow.'[25]

All the air crews were volunteers, but the reality behind their patriotic dreams of service caused more young men to suffer breakdowns than contemporary propaganda could admit, and their chance of surviving a tour of duty was barely fifty-fifty during the harshest bombing campaigns. The survivors, men like some of our friends and former colleagues, have lived most of their lives with such memories. We have never probed their responses to the dilemmas posed by their roles as members of the armed forces. The commitment of a nation to war inevitably blurs the dividing line between our notions of morality and immorality and members of the forces have no right to question decisions made by their commanders.

The contrast between the recollected emotions of my younger self and the preserved realities represented by these later experiences has made me reflect frequently on my position now as a woman in her eighties looking into images from the mind of the child, the schoolgirl, the young adult. It has been a strange journey, from the baby in the pram to the university student, reclaimed from that enigma we call memory. Such recollections

---

[25] Hastings, *Bomber Command*, 90.

are selective, subject to interpretation, and represent sharp visual images from that minute and unpredictable area of everyday experience which is sufficiently impressive as it occurs to be stored for future recall. The fascinating thing is that they exist simultaneously; the village of that name and its school are there to be seen and visited, but few people living there now remember the cottages opposite the school. My village of the 1930s exists only as a living, vulnerable memory, along with my first sight, in 1943, of the house and fields at Upper Dunsforth which were to be my home for twenty-six years from 1958, the latter then closely grazed by cattle right up to the farm buildings. The lanes are there still, but many of their wayside flowers are gone and the fields are managed differently; the affluent inhabitants, fiercely defensive of 'their' village, with its estates of comfortable houses and its luxuriously extended cottages, belong to the new century. The skies are as lovely on a summer evening, but the planes silhouetted there are bound for or returning to regional airports, full of holiday-makers or business travellers, or flying over to distant destinations, their bright, high vapour trails lingering and dissolving behind them.

In Leeds, the University is as familiar in memory as in its present form. Alongside those who tote huge rucksacks and water bottles and mobile phones and, like me, work at their laptops, the Brotherton Library can echo strangely with whispers from the past, be peopled again with those who never grow old, some of whom, like Chris and Joan and almost certainly Georg, are already dead. Oxley Hall has seen generations of students and their Oxley bears little resemblance to mine. Like us, they have lived and fallen in love there and moved on. Geoff and I are among the few older people who returned to the university of the 1980s to take higher degrees. We stayed to make other friends and use it as a happy working environment.

It is no wonder, when we carry with us such a panorama stretching back and changing over the years, that we reflect on it as older people and evoke our memories to re-evaluate current experience, or just enjoy the relaxation of recollection, as I have done for much of the time in writing this. It becomes even more important, though, not to be sucked into the dream, not to close one's mind to the significance of the present and future in the pleasure of re-creating a bygone world. For me, there are still things to be written, new skills to be learned, new experiences to be enjoyed and always there is the beckoning finger as if we were permanently here to create our realities from the raw material of everyday life.

I wondered if this sustained recollection would finally lay to rest that yearning to live again in the countryside, to seek the old magic by moving to another village, where I could breathe fresh, fragrant air and gaze out every day of my old age onto a lovely landscape and broad acres rather than onto a small garden in a Leeds suburb, the last place in which I would have expected ultimately to find satisfaction, even peace and contentment, for what always will be a restless spirit. It has done just that, because I know now that I am where I should be, where Geoff and I can find all that we need for happiness, and can delight in the experiences which bring quiet enjoyment to every day that we share.

The village of my childhood, like the way of life it represented, is gone, and the world I knew, full of the scents and sounds of an earlier rural society cannot be recreated in any other place. The villages glimpsed from a train, the fields with cattle and horses, the hedgerows, and solitary trees standing in open pasture land, will always raise an echo of the way life used to be and if they bring a lump in my throat, it is of happy reflection only tinged with regret. The past is always there in the present, the panorama of life as it has already been lived. While memory lasts, nothing can separate me from that bygone village; it is in me and shaped me, as did the university of the forties, the seventies, the eighties and nineties, the travels to other countries, including Germany where we shared with our friends in Erfurt a performance in English of Benjamin Britten's *War Requiem,* a moving experience for all of us as we heard the immortal words from *Strange Meeting,* ' I am the enemy you killed, my friend', and thought of all that had happened and what might have been. Above all our family are part of this panorama of life and past life; the girls who became women, their children in turn joining the uncertain, unfolding daily pattern of adult experience and family life, and our great-grandchildren, the next generation, taking their first experimental steps into the lifelong adventure. They continually lead me deeper into the mystery and art of living; I am humbled by their varied skills and wisdom and apprehensive, too, about what the future may hold, particularly for the younger members who will live on in an unpredictable world that my generation will never know.

Having returned for a while with pleasure, excitement, yes, sadness too, and recalled those early years with their ambiguities, and seen again the people who surrounded me and helped to shape my life, still vividly alive to me in their full humanity as I perceived it then, I cherish the memory of times past. This rich resource helps me to find a compassion, tolerance and respect for other people which I never had as a younger woman. By accepting it as a source of understanding rather than nostalgic regret I have found a new freedom to meet the future creatively, comparatively short as it must be and whatever it may hold. Everyday life in its variety and fragility, its joys and sorrows, its experience of human suffering and resilience, is beautiful in the deepest meaning of the word; it is precious and a great responsibility. For me it is still full of new experiences, new friendships, new insights into what it means to be human; it is immeasurably good.